The Perfect Gift of a Mother

AKINDOTUN MERINO, PhD

The Perfect Gift of a Mother

TATE PUBLISHING
AND ENTERPRISES, LLC

Published by Tate Publishing & Enterprises, LLC
127 E. Trade Center Terrace | Mustang, Oklahoma 73064 USA
1.888.361.9473 | www.tatepublishing.com

Tate Publishing is committed to excellence in the publishing industry. The company reflects the philosophy established by the founders, based on Psalm 68:11,
"The Lord gave the word and great was the company of those who published it."

Cover design by Nino Carlo Suico
Interior design by Jomar Ouano

Published in the United States of America

ISBN: 978-1-68207-210-3
1. Family & Relationships / Parenting / Motherhood
2. Self-Help / Personal Growth / General
16.01.19

WHAT OTHERS ARE SAYING

God's vision of motherhood in all its intricacies (spiritual, physical, emotional). This is a well-rounded, well written book on all aspects of motherhood from a Godly perspective.

—Dr. Kitty Bickford, DBS, CPC
Founder, Pasture Valley Children Missions and Benevolence

Akin posit that women should follow seven stages to prove significance. Among them are preparing to have a vision, the fight for the dream, the fertilization stage, the incubation stage and the birthing stage. The qualities of significant mothers are also highlighted which gives motivation to every woman who wants to live a life of significance. Prayers and confession were introduced as tools for developing influence. The most amazing chapter was how she juxtaposed scriptures and Erik Erikson's developmental stages to guide parents. Powerful women are definitely tripartite beings who utilize spirit, soul, and body to demonstrate God's goodness.

—Dr. Loretta Kiel

The gift of a mother is a powerful instructional book written by Dr. Akin Merino. It is the balance of scriptures, physiology and insightful revelations on the importance of women in birthing dreams. The author sites various biblical references as examples of women who shaped events in their world negatively or positively. She celebrates the fact that motherhood is replete with creative abilities. There is an amazing chapter on the concept of a perfect fit between men and women as the original plan for a marriage relationship. Women raise concerns in cases where their children are exposed to dangers similar to Rachel wailing, a symbol for all women who are inconsolable when children are destroyed. Women are instrumental in helping birth the spiritual, careers and financial aspirations of their children.

—Laura Milicevic
A Tutorial fellow at African Nazarene University (ANU)
Nairobi, Kenya

A significant book on the role of women! They are presented as the arbiter of blessings and grace for progeny and legacies. If you are itching for a change or need an understanding of the mechanisms of success, this is the book for you.

—Pastor Ilean Frasier
Second Wind Ministries

To all the significant women in my life.
To my children who make life a miracle.
To the love of my life—the one who deepens my story!

Son, behold, your mother!

The Vision

Build a company of significant women.

Contents

1 The Woman of Destiny 13
2 The Perfect Fit 19
3 Attack the Child: Awaken the Lioness 29
4 Seven Stages of Significance 37
5 The Significant Mother 59
6 Her Calling 63
7 Three-Part Being 83
8 Her Body 89
9 Her Intercession 101
10 Her Action 115
11 Her Courage 125
12 Her Commitment 131
13 Her Private Victories 165
14 Her Successes 169
15 Her Education 179

16 Her Business 183
17 Her Rejuvenation 189
18 Her Support 197

Appendix 201
Notes 203

1

The Woman of Destiny

Significant: "having or expressing meaning"

We cannot understand mothers until we understand a woman. A woman is the individual created with a womb. A woman is the crowning glory of creation and is a significant part of the divine plan. Women sometimes allow themselves to be defined by standards enacted by others. Some women are exploited, abused, maligned, misused, yet they keep on believing for a better day. The questions from the Creator are: Where are my daughters? Where are the Deborahs of this age? Where are the tenacious Ruths? Where are my bold Esthers? A response resounds in the aisles of cities and homes: Some of them are single, waiting to be betrothed. Some are mothers caring for little ones. Some are wives waiting for husbands to come home. Some are professionals working the corporate ladder or holding down jobs. Some are young and in school. Some are brokenhearted, cast down, and forsaken. Some are wounded soldiers knocked down a level or two in the battle we call church. They are all, however, daughters of destiny.

Who has lied to us about the meaning of life? Who is keeping us at the fringes of the kingdom? Who had the audacity to call what came out of perfection "second class"? Why are we finding significance in lifeless places? When the women went into the tomb searching for Jesus on resurrection morning, the angel asked them a pertinent question, "Why are you searching for the living among the dead?' The paradoxical reality of that moment was that women (living) were standing at that moment in a tomb (dead). This is the story of all of us at some point. We are living in joyless homes, struggling in dead marriages and in hopeless jobs, raising children in times of chaos while trying to maintain sanity.

The Voice of Acceptance

> The woman is the crowning glory of creation. My life gave you life. Man and woman he created them (Genesis 1:27). You are mine. You are a spirit, created in the image and likeness of your father. I gave you life. I gave you meaning. You are accepted. You are bigger than your problems. I am calling my daughters.

Woman was created mother from the very beginning. She was made to create life. She is a vital part of this system.

Motherhood is glorious and supernatural. The ability to carry and reproduce life makes women co-creators. The power inherent in every woman is evident in our ability to conceive and birth children. You are supposed to keep recreating in spiritual and physical spaces. This book is about the glory and power of mothering—what it means and how to positively impact lives from your home. Understanding the role of mothers and why you are undeniably necessary in the kingdom of God. Mothers were made to naturally enjoy supernatural experiences.

"Then He said, 'Let Us Make man in our image and in our likeness'" (Genesis 1:26). He made them male and female just like himself. A woman is as much like God as the man. She is not lower or less significant. She is the image of her father. A woman looks just like God.

When the Creator addressed man in Genesis 1:28, he was simultaneously speaking to woman as well. Their assignments basically were to be fruitful and multiply. The Hebrew word for fruitful is *parah*, "to bring forth, to bear fruit." He gave the same commission to the land, air, and sea creatures: they were to replenish the earth by recreating their own kind. Adam was created a father and Eve was created a mother.

He also gave them another commission to multiply. Multiply here does not mean the same as fruitful in Hebrew. Multiply means *rabah*, which means "to increase in authority; to bring up; grow up; multiply; nourish." God further told them to have dominion. What he was saying to mother and father is that they were to continue the work of creation by using all the resources that were at their disposals to continue the work of creation that was starting in the beginning. Eve was to be the constant reminder to humanity that the creative power of God is still at work in them. They were supposed to keep recreating the Garden of Eden till the whole earth was filled with the glory of their Father.

Women have a history of displacement and inequity. During the feminist movement, women went to the extreme of competing with men, instead of finding meaning in womanhood. We now have a generation of young girls who will never know what it is like to be cared for by a male. Traditional niceties like opening the door, pulling out your chair, standing up when you walk in the room, and paying for your meals have become obsolete. This is the bill of rights we've sold our daughters and they will suffer for it. It is not about lifting big boxes or opening doors, it is that we have misunderstood and misinterpreted our commission as women. On the other hand, there are women who won't do anything with their lives, who have relegated their authority to others.

Adam was created first and part of his specific assignment was to administer the work of creation. He realized he needed companionship and a vision carrier to birth God's mandate. He wanted human fellowship and the

Creator took some parts of him to create the woman. He was a complete man until his female part was taken from him. God found a way to make these two come together to fit perfectly.

When the woman was finally realized, God formed her physical features differently because He wanted her to administer the work of creation differently. Man had experienced creation by taking a physical part in it, but when God designed Eve, He wanted her participation to be more intimate. He designed the reproductive organs, the belly, and the breasts that would invariably help her birth children. The woman mirrored his creative powers on the earth. She is the vessel through which His missions and purposes would be unfolded and realized in this world. He commissioned the woman to be another agent of power (like her husband) in this world.

2

The Perfect Fit

When two elements come together that are exactly adapted or suitable to each other. To be the precise size and shape for.

The first husband and wife were a perfect fit, which means that they were perfectly suited for each other, lacking nothing essential to their union, whole and complete. Adam and Eve were the physical manifestation of the peace (Shalom) of God—nothing missing or broken. Adam recognized Eve as his own. "Bone of my bone and flesh of my flesh." This was the woman he would be joined to for the rest of his life. The first test of perfect fit is recognition. When you meet the woman who will become the mother of your children, you will recognize her. You will feel like this is home. Jacob recognized Rachel right away in the twenty-ninth book of the beginnings. The verse said that Jacob kissed Rachel and lifted up his voice and wept. He had ran hundreds of miles for fear of his life. He had left with nothing more than a blessing and a sack lunch. He was weary. Jacob was hungry. He had been pursued. He had lost more than he gained. He had no place to call home, but as soon as Rachel arrived, he recognized why he had been separated for so long. He knew that this was his perfect fit. The person to whom his destiny was tied.

They were partners, one that is united or associated with another or others in an activity or a sphere of common interest. They had a mandate from the Lord to be fruitful and to multiply. It is therefore important for the man to have a sense of purpose because the woman is united with him in purpose of a common interest. Adam as the king and she as the queen of their kingdom.

They were naked and unashamed. That means that they communicated on multiple levels. They understood and knew each other. They were naked, which means there were no secrets. Adam shared his deeper self with her and Eve did the same. They were naked in their desires and needs. They were stripped of all trepidations. They were not trying to prove anything to each other. They shared micro and macro conversations of the type of kingdom they would build and the burden of the tree of knowledge of good and evil. I believe that Adam as the king of the kingdom became frustrated about the command not to eat the forbidden fruit of the tree. After all, the kingdom was given to him and he should have authority over all of it.

These were conversations that the man and woman had in the garden which gave room for the adversary to enter their kingdom. Women are the incubators and deliverers of purpose. They will birth desires of the man. The woman was deceived in thinking she could disobey and remain in the garden. She was also deceived into thinking her actions would only impact the micro and not the entire mankind. Eve, like any other woman, was birthing her husband's desire. This would explain how the scripture says that she gave him the apple and he ate. This is the action of two people in partnership. Adam knew that this single act of disobedience was for him. This position is validated by the punishment meted out to the woman. The Lord said that her husband will rule over her. Why? Because she yielded to the wishes of her husband instead of the command of the Lord.

They fit physically. There are many problems that can keep a woman from enjoying sex. They include:

- Lack of sexual desire
- Inability to become aroused
- Lack of orgasm, or sexual climax
- Painful intercourse

These problems may have physical or psychological causes. Physical causes may include conditions like diabetes, heart disease, nerve disorders, or hormone problems. Some drugs can also affect desire and function. Psychological causes may include work-related stress and anxiety. They may also include depression or concerns about marriage or relationship problems. For some women, the problem results from past sexual trauma. However, I believe that the primary reason for most sexual problems is that people are not with their perfect fit. When you are not with the right person, sex can be very good, but it would not have the natural awe. The penis is supposed to caress the walls of your vagina bringing you to climax. About 75 percent of all women never reach orgasm from intercourse alone—that is, without the extra help of sex toys, hands, or tongue. And 10 to 15 percent never climax under any circumstances.

I believe that Adam's penis was shaped, sized, and measured to perfectly fit Eve's vagina. It is perfectly built to stimulate and bring her to orgasm without gadgets and medication. The joining of man and woman was meant to be an awesome experience; it is a place we experience heaven on earth. Children were conceived in such atmosphere, and Eve became the mother of the living.

In the Beginning…

God was "pregnant" with the picture of a heaven and earth filled with light and beauty. God's pregnancy is witnessed by the Spirit moving or brooding upon the surface of the earth (Genesis 1: 2). The word *brood* means "flutter, move, or shake." This is like the pregnancy experience of a mother.

After the pregnancy had come to full term, then God spoke. Just like a woman delivers a baby, so also we need to deliver the dreams that we carry in our hearts. The woman is created to bring to birth.

The purpose of the Spirit moving over the face of the waters was to give life to the vision. It was a gestation period for the Father. We don't know how long it was for Him, but we do know that it normally takes nine months for a woman. God didn't create anything until after the Spirit had nursed His vision. He had the dream of a different world, a new world complete with mankind in his belly. Once the dream had matured, then God spoke. So, the woman was designed to keep the creation process going through eternity. What an awesome responsibility! The woman was a vital part of this process.

We are women on a mission. We are to use this gift to birth and raise children. How can we limit the Creator who took time and extraordinary care in forming us as his crowning glory? He basically said, "This woman would help unfold my vision in this world. She is to become the mission bearer for future generations."

Satan's original intention was to destroy this mandate through the woman. She was a powerful instrument in the hands of the Father, and if he could distort that, then he would have managed to stop creation. It had nothing to do with the semantics of whom God gave the command to or not. It had to do with being co-creators. It had to do with the world as we know it coming to a stand still. If the mother could be done away with, then everything ceases. Adam had proven that he couldn't complete the vision without her help.

It is no wonder that the mother has been undervalued, displaced, degraded, and devalued in our world. Nothing can replace the gift that was bestowed upon her in the beginning. The gift to birth life is too precious to relegate. Not enough of us realize the power of this mission, but when we do, we become "significant."

We've heard that Eve was deceived, and I posit that her error was triggered by the need to birth desires. We know that the man and woman in the beginning were naked and unashamed, which means that they had openness. They didn't hide anything from each other. The serpent was let into that garden by the man who had struggled with the godly command of not touching the tree of the knowledge of good and evil. This must have been discussed with his wife who was his help meet. It was just a matter of time before Eve brought the desires of her husband's heart to pass. Have you ever wondered why Adam never questioned Eve when she brought him the fruit? Well, it was because this was a culmination of past conversations and desires. Women were created to bring things to pass. The man and woman later experienced the consequences of their actions. The woman's punishment is that her desire will be to her husband because that was the desire she tried to meet in the first place. He will rule over her because she forgot to love the Lord more than her husband. It is only in Christ that women are returned to their original status. The place of the woman is not behind her husband but next to him. It is in Christ that women are repositioned.

Significant mothers understand this power and tap into it to transcend life's circumstances. You cannot be the woman you were created to be if you don't understand why you were created. You are here on a mission. Consider yourself a co-creator. When you are pregnant with those babies, what you are doing is allowing the Lord to use your body as an instrument through which another soul is deposited into this world. We are joint creators when we nurse our children and raise them into adulthood. We train and nurture lives for the kingdom.

You are a God helper. He needs us to keep reproducing dreams, unveiling light, manifesting life, and bringing deliverance to our world.

Watson, the behavioral psychologist, underscored this idea of the power inherent in motherhood through this quote:

> Give me a dozen healthy infants, well-formed, and my own specified world to bring them up in and I'll guarantee to take any one at random and train him to become any type of specialist I might select—doctor, lawyer, artist, merchant-chief, and, yes, even beggarman and thief, regardless of his talents,

> penchants, tendencies, abilities, vocations, and race of his ancestors. I am going beyond my facts and I admit it, but so have the advocates of the contrary and they have been doing it for many thousands of years. (John B. Watson, *Behaviorism*, 1930)

The only difference is that for a Christian mother, this statement is not exaggerated or oversimplified. You have been endowed with the power to shape the lives of communities and nations through the children that you raise.

He designed it that way. Some people say that God doesn't need anybody, that he is God all by Himself. I agree with the last part—God is omnipotent, omniscient, omnipresent, and transcendent. God made himself in need of fallible mankind by putting them in charge of his creation. He needed Moses to lead the Israelites. He needed the Harlot Rahab for the deliverance of Israeli spies. God is definitely in need of a woman. He is searching for someone whose heart is perfect toward him. God wants us to be dependent on him, as he is dependent on us to fulfill his will in this world. He is surely in need of mothers.

Therefore, you must realize that the power to create another life is infinite. You have the power to create life. Most women understand that giving birth is one of the natural miracles of our lifetime. What they do not understand is that all the other stressors that compound our roles as women distract us from continuing the same process in other areas of life. We unfortunately make other things in our lives more important than the original mission. The same creative power manifested in the birthing of your child is supposed to be evident in all areas of your life. Imagine what will happen to our world if mothers suddenly took their position's authority.

A significant mother is one who brings life to everything around her including herself, husband, children, and community. Just as your womb is full of children, so also is your heart full of visions. The significant mother uses the same process of birthing to manifest dreams and visions. Mothers should be birthing their desires for peace, joy, tranquility, and prosperity in their homes and lives. The Father has downloaded these visions into your heart. He desires to express Himself through the mother. Jesus came to restore women back to their position of authority. He released the divorcee into the evangelistic ministry; He honored the single women, the depressed, the wealthy. He addressed them when all the rabbis considered them second-class citizens, not to be recognized. The woman is the expressed image of the Father. She was made to declare his intention for creation. She is the Mission Bearer.

3

Attack the Child: Awaken the Lioness

> A cry was heard in Ramah—weeping and great mourning. Rachel weeps for her children, refusing to be comforted, for they are dead. (Matthew 2:18)

The wailing of Rachel is the most excruciating and piercing cry in the universe. Mothers wailing for their children who are lost, stolen, abandoned, suffering, addicted, prostituting, aborted, killed, murdered, and swallowed up by the powers of drugs, poverty, legal, abuse, and other "Pharaohs" who have sent a contract out for the destruction of children. Mothers wail in lonely abandonments or in anxious groups lamenting the plight of these lost children. We were made to take care of the offspring as the arbiter of goodness and mercy. When things disintegrate, our fabric begins to unravel and the foundations of the world become unstable. This book makes no distinction between married, divorced, adopted, foster, single and never married, young, middle age, or elderly mothers. Once a child is entrusted in your care as the primary caregiver, you have joined the ranks of Eve, powerful mothers who will change the world.

Whenever the child is wounded, the lioness is awakened. We heard that a student had committed suicide at a high school in my neighborhood and a prayer meeting was called the next Saturday. Do you know who showed up? Mothers! We not only care for our own, we care for the children of the world.

Mothers are the solution. Candy Lightner founded Mothers against Drunk Driving (MADD) in 1980 after her daughter, Cari, was killed by a repeat drunk driving offender. Cindy Lamb—whose daughter, Laura, became the nation's youngest quadriplegic at the hands of a drunk driver—soon joined Candy in her crusade to save lives.

While a military junta ruled Argentina from 1976 to 1983, dissent was silenced. In broad daylight or in the middle of the night, dissidents were swept from their homes, and across the nation those who spoke suddenly "disappeared," either to prison with torture or the grave. It became dangerous to socialize with those who spoke out against the military. The silence was broken by a brave group of mothers, searching for their missing children. At the first demonstration on April 30, 1977, only fourteen women participated, but by the following year hundreds were participating.

Jenni Williams became one of the founders of Woza, a grassroots opposition movement created in response to a perceived lack of action by Zimbabwe's men against the Mugabe government. The organization focused on public mass protests against Mugabe, and grew to seventy thousand members in the following years.

The lioness has been awakened all throughout history and they have roared back in mighty ways. There are several qualities of a lioness that the woman possesses.

The lioness is sultry and svelte: She is self confident and assured. She understands her place within the family. She exudes beauty and acceptance. She will nurture and protect. She walks with poise and is strategic in her hunting. So are you, lioness woman! There is no one else like you. You should have a healthy dose of sense of self as you are surrounded by other lionesses.

The lioness lives with her sisters: Family matters to her and is the epitome of "it takes a village." Mothers can learn to harness strength in numbers like the lioness. We can teach and guide younger mothers. If someone with experience had told me when I was nursing my firstborn that the initial pain of breastfeeding will cease and would be followed by the incredible bonding with your child, I would have been a little bit more patient during that process.

The lioness hunts for the pride, which means that she provides the food. We are told that the Proverbs 31 woman wakes up early to prepare food for her household. Mothers also nurture, feeding their children physically and in other areas, like emotionally, socially, and so on. A great hunter must have great patience, clarity, and timing. Mothers must exercise great patience with their children. Pray for clarity and hunt for resources to help your children to excel in their world. We provide nutrition for our homes. Let us not allow things that will damage our children's future into the house.

The lioness has intention. This is a powerful quality. The mother must understand the goals and pursuits of her family. This can be discussed as a family or as individuals. A family that has no intention is like driving without a destination. We could end up anywhere. We must be intent on the trajectory of our lives as a family. Some intentions are:

- Creating a spiritual space: Praying as a family and studying the scriptures.
- Time together: This includes eating together, traveling, games.
- Giving: Families who learn to give early reveal God to others since he is a giver
- Communication: Discuss life issues, history, news, developmental stages, money matters, marriage, dating, politics, religion, relationship. Tell them how you feel about issues. Create an atmosphere that allows the children to converse with you openly.

What do we stand for in this family and what are we against?

____

____

What is our mission and how do we accomplish it?

____

____

The lioness is protective. She will protect all the cubs in the pride. We are mothers to those in the house, but we are also mothers to children of the world. If women lose sight of this awesome responsibility, the foundation of the world will be toppled. We are to protect each child and all other children. We should pass laws that protect. Jesus brought the children close enough to himself to lay hands upon them. Let us bring children closer so they are not destroyed by predators in the land. The lioness roars when the cubs are in danger. Lionesses also roar together when their cubs are threatened, which means that women should advocate for the children in their communities.

What is your living desire for your children?

Example Goals

- **Spiritual:** To live a spiritual existence by having a personal relationship with the trinity, be part of the Household of Faith, and understand the transcendent power of spirit.

- **Emotional:** To live a healthy emotional existence with the ability to love and live peacefully.
- **Family:** Learn how to live within the context of family.
- **Career:** To understand the purpose of his/her existence and transform society through work.
- **Physical:** Make healthy decisions in terms of food, exercise, and presenting their bodies as a living model.
- **Social**: Have influence.
- **Financial**: Understand wealth is an instrument of change.

It is your turn!

The Goals

Spiritual:

____

____

Emotional:

____

____

Family:

____

____

Career:

Physical:

Social:

Financial:

4

Seven Stages of Significance

The Scripture

> And He said, "The kingdom of God is as if a man should scatter seed on the ground, and should sleep by night and rise by day, and the seed should sprout and grow, he himself does not know how. For the earth yields crops by itself: first the blade, then the head, after that the full grain in the head. But when the grain ripens, immediately he puts in the sickle, because the harvest has come." (Mark 9:26-29)

Stage 1: Preparation

The preparation stage prepares you for a child. The matured female body is constantly being prepared for childbirth. Just as your body prepares for childbirth, so you must prepare for your other dreams.

An ova (egg) begins to mature in the ovary. At the same time, the uterus lining begins to thicken in preparation for the ova. After about fourteen days, ovulation takes place, sending the ova down the ovary duct (fallopian tube). The ova only survives for twenty-four hours.

If sexual intercourse takes place but a sperm cell does not reach the ova, then the ova dies and shortly after, menstrual flow (period) begins to restart the cycle.

Definition of Menstruation:

A discharging of blood, secretions, and tissue debris from the uterus that recurs in nonpregnant, breeding-age primate females at approximately monthly intervals and that is considered to represent a readjustment of the uterus to the nonpregnant state following proliferative changes accompanying the preceding ovulation (Merriam-Webster).

What does this mean?

Just like your body keeps readjusting to the fertilization cycle, your life will readjust to unfulfilled dreams until you start incubating life dreams. Sometimes during midlife, we begin to realize the death of most dreams.

> Unrelenting disappointment leaves you heartsick, but a sudden good break can turn life around. (Proverbs 13:12, The Message)

What happened to the vision of your son or daughter becoming a dancer, artist, teacher, missionary, pastor, or to own the nonprofit shelter? As we struggle to raise these children and assist our husbands, many mothers, overwhelmed by the job, experience a constant flow of dream menstruation. "As arrows in the hand," we are supposed to understand the heart of destiny for our children. How we stir them determines where they will end up. We lose heart because visions seem to be slipping away from us. The draining of dreams can be stopped when we start investing in goodness. The good news is that menstruation is a sign that you are fertile. Your soul is still alive because you're experiencing loss. Your emptiness and loneliness will only be satisfied when you get pregnant with the Father's vision and purpose. Seek the Lord in prayer concerning your children and get the grand vision of how they will change the world. Your vision will become a mission.

> As for me and my children, we are for signs and wonders.

The task of this stage is preparation. This is the stage when most women, especially midlife women, start to ponder their lives and the legacy they'll leave behind. This is the stage where most of us start to question our existence. Why am I here? There must be more to life than this. What is the will of God concerning my life? What can I do to attain my dreams? Most healthy women don't remain too long in this stage because they have the innate ability to sense their calling which is intricately tied to the children. Dr. J. E. Kwegyir Aggrey, a visionary Ghanian educator, states that the surest way to keep a people down is to educate the men and neglect the women. If you educate a man, you simply educate an individual, but if you educate a woman, you educate a family. Unhealthy mothers spend a great deal of time agonizing at this stage because they are bombarded by the circumstances of their lives. They can't hear the whisper of the heart. So you want to dream again? What is your next step?

Make Room for the Vision

- Frequently set aside time to receive a refreshed vision. No one can get pregnant on yesterday's sperm.
- Allow the thrill of being able to change your world consume you.
- Spend time with the Father.
- Think about the vision. The act of meditation allows your vision to travel from your spirit to your soul and body.
- Write it down. The process of writing helps you clarify your thought process.
- Visualize the mission. The process of seeing before the actual manifestation is faith. If you can, get an illustration of your dream on paper.

- Understand the Mission Agent (you) has been specially equipped to birth this dream.
- Fall in love with the Father as you become passionate about the mission. You can't receive from someone you don't spend time with.

Stage 2: The Fight

During ejaculation, the sperm mature on their way to the uterus (womb). They enter the vagina and for about twenty minutes they cluster together, *while the female body attacks them*. About half the sperm die at this point due to increased temperature, or being attacked by the female's body defenses and the slightly higher acidic level. Sperm adapt to these changes and continue their journey to the ovary duct. Some sperm will never get anywhere near the ova as they are deformed, get stuck in tissue, go up the wrong ovary duct, or are removed when the penis is removed.

Very few sperm make it to the ovary duct. One ultimately reaches the ova, and the enzymes of this sperm allow it to penetrate the cell membrane of the ova. At this point, the ova membrane takes on a new form, trapping any other sperm getting any further. In nature, there is no such thing as a dead heat. Nature can always tell which sperm wins, no matter how little the difference. The nucleus of the sperm moves into the nucleus of the ova. This is called fertilization.

Not every vision is of God. Not every idea that comes into your mind is your vision. You cannot depend on your emotions because they are permeable. The visions that are from the Father will primarily emanate from a peaceful heart and bring illumination, reservation, and healing. This is the time when you need to fight for the dream you received from the Father. Fight your mind as it wants to vacillate from one thing to another, and fight circumstances that seek to keep you in a box. The cares of daily living will tend to choke up your visions if you let it, so you have to fight. The mission is bigger than you. When your vision is specific, it becomes a mission. All the resources of heaven will back your mission.

The mission is bigger than what you can accomplish by yourself. The mission we received from Jesus is to "go into all the world and make disciples of nations" (Matthew 28:19). God is called "The Desire of All Nations" (Haggai 2:7). All our individual visions must be connected to this one mission. Our audience is the world. We get to choose our part as we use the gifts and talents that have been given us. We have been commissioned for this kingdom. The apostle Paul admonished the Corinthian husband and wife to live with a focus on the kingdom work. Our time here on earth is limited. The mission was not just given to the man. Jesus, our master, promised that we will do greater things. Take inventory of your life and that of your children. Are you doing greater things? Are you assisting them in school, ensuring that they are registered for the correct courses, seeking assistance if you don't understand the process? Are they engaged in church and community or have you abdicated authority to the schools? Are you taking care of yourself to ensure that you are someone your children will be proud of? Do you make excuses because you are a mother? Staying in bathrobes all day, not combing your hair or reading a book for the past twelve years has no bearing on successful mothering. There is enough grace for us mothers to transform our families.

Fight for the Dream

- Commit to becoming a dreamer.
- Resist the temptation to overspread yourself.
- Understand that you are not a second-class citizen
- It's okay to say no even at church or work.
- Jesus came to release women into their destinies.

Stage 3: The Fertilization

The kingdom of God is as if a man should scatter
seed on the ground...

The sperm and egg unite in the fallopian tube to form a one-celled entity called a zygote. If more than one egg is released and fertilized, you may have multiple zygotes. The zygote has forty-six chromosomes—twenty-three from you and twenty-three from your partner. These chromosomes contain genetic material that will determine your baby's sex and traits such as eye color, hair color, height, facial features, and, at least to some extent, intelligence and personality.

Soon after fertilization, the zygote will travel down one of your fallopian tubes toward the uterus. At the same time, it will begin dividing rapidly to form a cluster of cells resembling a tiny raspberry. The inner group of cells will become the embryo. The outer group of cells will become the membranes that nourish and protect it.

Implantation

The zygote, by this time made up of about five hundred cells, is now known as a blastocyst. When it reaches your uterus, the blastocyst will burrow into the uterine wall for nourishment. The placenta, which will nourish your baby throughout the pregnancy, also begins to form. By the end of this week, you may be celebrating a positive pregnancy test.

Sex precedes pregnancy! Sexual intimacy can be really gratifying, but it is also work, time, and commitment. If a couple wants to get pregnant, they must take time out of their busy schedule to make love, or they make love because they are so intimate with each other. We are grateful for the enjoyment of sexual intercourse as it was God's design in the beginning. It was his way of ensuring that these two powerful entities would come together in the creating process. He could have had the first couple wish for a child or get children some other way, but He chose to design our bodies in such a way that the woman receives seed from the man. This is the way it should work with all our missions. They are to be downloaded into our spirits as we spend time with the Father.

The process of decision making to create a baby is that of commitment. Healthy mothers are making the choice every day to receive the seed of their dream, incubate it, and then give birth at the appropriate time. You must commit to the vision. It is a beautiful thing when pregnancy is a result of a healthy relationship, preferably marriage. Remember how you sat up with your spouse talking and dreaming about that first child, the product of your love? So also our vision should be a product of our relationship with the Father. The single act of committing to the mission transforms you into a significant mother. You are Eve, back in the garden with all the resources of life at your disposal. You have the ability to produce all the desires of your heart. Eve was given the same authority and access to the Father as her husband. You have the ability to enter the presence of the Father, and by spending time with him, his life will infuse your soul, and a mission will be born.

Intimacy with the Father

- Create time and spend time with the Father.
- The Father is in love with you. He loves you as much as He loves Jesus (John 17:23).
- Visualize yourself in the throne room of your daddy. What does he look like? How does he see you? The

Father is love. His very nature is bursting with love as you approach him. He yearns for this intimacy because he knows that's the only way to release seed inside you. He wants you to be the carrier of promise just as Mary was the carrier of the promise.

- The angel's message to Mary is true for every woman who will commit herself to living a significant life.
- You are highly favored. There is something about you that touches the Father's heart. You walk into the throne and he remembers his first intent for Woman. The angels stand at attention because here is another woman who dares to take on Eve's mantle.
- Worship is the act of sacrificing your life to the Father. We lie at the altar of his mercy and surrender our lives to him. The Father cannot do anything with the vision until he has your total allegiance. Just like your husband gave you a ring when you got married, the Father will partner with once he has your allegiance.
- This is an intensely intimate relationship for those women who dare to approach the throne.
- Plan for the mission. Just like you wouldn't have a child without preparing, so you should make plans for your mission.
- Make place or room for the mission. Sometimes your mission might entail you do something differently.

- Believe that you have been entrusted with a mission because the Father trusts you.

Stage 4: Transcendent Incubation

> ...and should sleep by night and rise by day, and the seed should sprout and grow, he himself does not know how...

Once you connect with the Father, a specific vision will be released into your heart. It is like being pregnant with your baby. It is a moment of joy and exhilaration. During pregnancy, we feel wistful and dreamy. Our thoughts are filled with promise and our emotions are heightened. Even though you cannot physically hold the baby, you feel the baby grow inside you as you nurture and help it grow. Of course, there are discomforts, but the idea of life within you quickly drives away the fears.

So now you have a purpose. What are you supposed to do with it? Every woman goes through three trimesters of pregnancy, just as your mission goes through these same stages. You're becoming a Significant.

First Trimester

> ...the earth yields crops by itself: first the blade...

During the first trimester, you can expect a host of pregnancy symptoms, including breast changes, tiredness, nausea and vomiting, frequent urination, and many more. At the end of the first trimester, your uterus will have grown to the size of a grapefruit, while the baby inside is the size of a cherry. The baby will grow from being a mass of cells to having a heartbeat, reflexes, and the ability to move its tiny limbs!

The first stage of transcendent incubation is the Symptomatic Stage. This is when you start getting epiphanies (light bulb moments) everywhere you go. You start having illumination as to how you can achieve the mission. You could be driving your car or cooking in the kitchen or be chairing an important meeting, when you suddenly get a thought as to how the mission can be fulfilled.

We usually receive one single direction at a time. The Bible tells us that the steps of righteous man are ordered by the Lord. So he will lead you one step at a time. This fosters dependency on him. If you are a type A personality like me, you will find this process incredibly frustrating. But we know that if we do things the kingdom way, we will have kingdom success.

This first stage of transcendent incubation will help you locate the how, when, and where. Since you spend time with the Father, he will drop ideas and suggestions into your heart or through people, things, and everything around you. You simply have to be attentive to the indicators of the mission. You will wake up in the middle of the night with specific directions. You might have to go out of your way to call or talk to somebody you don't know or want to speak to. You might be asked to do things that don't make sense. What if you have a feeling that you should go speak to your next-door neighbor who you haven't spoken to in a while? Will you ignore it or get out of your comfort zone and take a risk? It is the most important period of the incubation of this dream. The Father will lead you to people who will help you grow the dream. It might mean filling out applications or writing letters to schools and various organizations. It might mean walking in love and forgiving those that have wronged you. It could mean meeting other parents in the neighborhood. The best thing I know to do during this period is seeding.

Start planting seed for your mission. Help your children fulfill a mission. Remember, what you make happen for others, God will make happen for you. The book of Ecclesiastes 11:1-3a (NLT) states:

> Give generously, for your gifts will return to you later. Divide your gifts among many, for you do not know what risks might lie ahead. When the clouds are heavy, the rains come down.

The principle of sowing and reaping necessitate that if you keep giving, harvest is bound to follow. This is a kingdom principle. Since we are embarking on a kingdom mission, we must use kingdom principles. We keep giving until the clouds are heavy enough to pour down rain. So during this time, seek ways to give. Become more generous to your loved ones and strangers; your children will learn how to give. Be nice to the teller at the bank or checker who is having a bad day; your children will learn kindness. Feed a poor child and pay for somebody's tuition; you are seeding for your children. Be kind and generous; and someone else will be kind and generous to your children. Remember, everything you sow is laying up treasures in your heavenly account which is usually cashed here on earth. It is only stored in heaven so that you will have something to draw upon when needed.

Intimacy with the Father

- Become sensitive to the ideas and information you are about to receive. Once you understand your mission, heaven and earth will move to help you fulfill it.
- Decide not to be lazy. Most people kill their dreams at this stage because they are too lazy to triage the symptoms. You must get aggressive and move when you're supposed to.
- Continue writing in your journal. Write down what you're feeling or what you need to do. If your dream is to go back to school and you still have little kids at home, don't settle for a lie that you can't do it now. You are a significant mother. Do not feel bogged down, intimidated, and guilty because you want to do other things. You can do all things through the

strength of Jesus in you. So ask him for ideas. How can you do this? I decided to go back to school for my doctorate while I was pregnant with my last child. I still had to fill out applications, financial aid forms, letters of recommendations, etc. I wouldn't have my doctorate degree today if I had missed out on those few simply steps.

- The first trimester is foundational and instrumental to you realizing your dreams.
- You must nurture the vision by getting all you need to fulfill it. If it is purchasing a business, call a broker or friend who can help you. If it is starting a nonprofit, find out how you can do it. If it is having a good marriage, find out what you need to do. If it is making sure your children get into college, then find out how you can help them. Remember, the vision should make your life and that of those around you better. You can have it all in Christ.
- Become focused. Don't get sidetracked. If the dream is to go back to school or write a book, you cannot commit yourself to other unnecessary things. You cannot be the school mom, let someone else do that. You cannot do all the laundry yourself; there is nothing wrong with your kids or husband helping. On the other hand, if they are too little, learn to live with the mess until you are able to load the laundry.

Second Trimester

...then the head...

Throughout the second trimester, your belly will start to show the baby growing inside you. You'll experience pregnancy discomforts such as sleeping problems and notice Braxton Hicks contractions. During the second trimester, your baby will grow hair all over its body and the senses will begin to develop. At the end of the second trimester, your baby will measure about ten inches (25 cm) and will frequently practice their kicking movements.

You are moving beyond the foundation stage here. You are now growing your vision. You've applied to correspondence school, started taking cooking lessons and volunteering at the homeless shelter, or taken parenting classes to become a better mom. The vision is growing. You have decided to start the business, written your business plan, and gone to all the right people. You are on track.

The problem with most women who suffer from low self-esteem is that they have never done anything spectacular. Your low self-esteem is intricately tied to your children's lack of self. While your mission is for others, it also helps your own self-image. When you get to this stage, you will discover that your self-esteem is increasing. You will dress better. Your children, husband, family, and friends will take note and comment on this new person in the family.

You will be like the light that was spoken of which cannot be hid.

Problems at this Stage

- Jealousy. People close to you might have helped you in stage 1, but once you get to stage 2, they will start getting scared. They wonder if you're still going to be the same wife or mother or sister or friend. They are insecure, so they might either withdraw from you or try to talk you out of your mission. So be cognizant of mission killers.
- Self-Pride. You start becoming important to yourself. You become obnoxious and intolerable.
- Disorganized. You will not be able to achieve your dream if you get disorganized with your time and schedules.
- Distance from the Father. Because there is so much activity at this stage, you might find yourself drifting away from the "Abba, Father."

Solutions

- Meditation. Find alone time, which might be your bathroom at this time in your life. Meditate on the goodness and awesomeness of the Father. Have conversations and permit Him to speak back to you. Meditate on the word by selecting a scripture relevant to your vision. Ponder it in your mind.

Think about it over and over again. Ask the Spirit to reveal the intent of that scripture to you. As you meditate, you will receive deeper meanings and truths that will strengthen you for the work ahead.

- Pray for the people around you. You have to cut off some of the negative sources, but others like your husband and children can be brought into the vision. Just like the angel had to inform Joseph about Mary's pregnancy, God will also take care of your spouse. Ask God to send him or them a visitation if they are resistant. I believe every family should have a mission that is big enough for everyone. Remember, you are there to either help jump start or fulfill a mission. God is not the author of confusion. The mission is big enough and diverse enough to require you as an individual or a wife, mother, daughter, etc. Don't be afraid, if God gave it to you, He will move heaven and earth to make sure it comes to fruition. Remember God calls women. He is calling you. When he calls you, he will empower you.
- Fellowship. Spend time with the important people in your life. Your job at this time is to spend time with your spouse and explain to him and the children what you are about to do. Ask them for help and they will. If you find a very resistant spouse, it's usually because they feel or think they will become neglected. Communication and prayer

is very important to getting their blessing. Wives need to ask for wisdom and prudence. Don't become combative but ask him in love.

- Stand. After having done all you can to protect the vision, keep standing!

Third Trimester

...after that the full grain in the head...

The third trimester brings many changes to your body. You will need to urinate frequently and your belly looks like it's ready to explode. Now is the time to start preparing for childbirth.

You have worked hard to plan this, vision, and it's time to birth it. It's time to get the book published. It's time to send the children off to summer camp or baby sitter for a couple of hours so you can attend classes. It's time to watch your teenager move on to college. It's time to start selling those cookies you've labored so hard to bake. It's time to start a homeless shelter. It's time to join the school board. It's time to take your child on a trip to Europe. It's time to move into that house and stop paying someone else's rent. It's time to be delivered from all the past pains. It's time to be set free. It's time to ask for the promotion. It's time to dictate your own hours and pay. It's time to graduate. It's time to become a voice for the hopeless. It's time to make a difference in another person's life. Basically, it's time to become undeniable! It's time, but it's not right now. You have to wait for birth bangs. You must wait for a little bit—it's God's work. You must expect a miracle. You must birth it at the right time. You're almost there. Expect a miracle!

Last Stage of Preparation

- Take ownership of the mission by accepting responsibility and committing to its success.
- Dedicate it to the Father. Allow him to breathe new life into your mission.
- Now wait for the precise time.
- Be appreciative.
- Show mercy to others who have tolerated you and helped you come this far.
- Be aware of final stage transition. Quite a number of missions are terminated at this point. You just simply ask all those who started PhD programs and end up with ABDs (All But Dissertation). Why do they come this far to give up? Well, because two things happen to you when you get to the finish line—either you get a burst of energy or you are depleted of energy. Just ask any athlete, the final lap is the most difficult. You need a focal point; a fan or fans to cheer you on. You need a reason to finish.
- Surround yourself with other significant women. Find people or one person who will be your cheerleader during this time.

- Keep on moving even if it feels cumbersome. The end is soon to come.

Stage 5: Birthing

> …But when the grain ripens, immediately he puts in the sickle, because the harvest has come.
>
> As soon as Zion travailed she brought forth her children. (Isaiah 66:8)

It's time for the delivery. You are having birth pangs. The manuscript has been finished. It's opening day for the business. This is your season. You've been planning this mission for a long time. It's time to see the fruits of your labor. The sad news is that most people never birth their dreams. The birthing process needs a new wave of strength unlike the one used during the pregnancy. The adversary wants to sabotage everything you've worked so hard for. He doesn't want to see women reflecting the glory of the Creator. Commissioner. He will not rest until he makes you another casualty of war. You will hear statements like, "Who does she think she is?" "Women are not supposed to be in ministry." "She cannot really be a pastor." "God just wants you to lead this small group of women." "You cannot expect a publisher to publish that book." Whose report will you believe? Remember, if you listen to them and get distracted or derailed, the Father will ask you the same question he asked Eve, "Who have you been listening to?"

You are not average. Whatever you deliver is for this kingdom. You are not only laying treasures for the nations, you are stocking up your heavenly account. Since the foundation of the world, the enemy has been working hard to disrupt the position of women while the Father has been restoring women to their place of authority. Listen to Jesus. Watch how he restored women to their position of dignity. You have given your life meaning. You've stepped into your significance!

5

The Significant Mother

In the book of Proverbs chapter 31, the king wrote this poem based upon the strong advice from his mother. It is his vision of a powerful woman. Who can compete with the Proverbs 31 woman? Her strength is overwhelming, her power is transfixing, her influence is contagious. Who can really measure up to her? She takes cares of her family and manages servants She has her own business as a fashion designer. Where does she get the strength? If you are like me, you can hardly find time to get dressed, much less make one. This is a woman who intimidates all the others.

Yet, I hear the answer to my question loud and clear. The powerful Proverbs 31 woman walked in the Father's original intention and so shines her light for the world to see. We, too, are powerful. We are royalty. We have the attention of the king. We are a special group of women, powerful in our calling and resolute in our pursuit. We create power in our environment and everything we touch becomes significant.

There are others just like this woman in the canvas of Scripture. There is Sarah, who protected the promise of her son Isaac by getting rid of Ishmael and his mother. Rebekah conspired to hasten the blessings of God for the chosen one, Jacob. The two mothers, Leah and Rachel, birthed the budding kingdom.

What can I say of Jochebed, who gave birth to three mighty warriors—Miriam, Aaron, and Moses? She showed strength and courage when she released her boy Moses, so that she might save his life. Her trust in Yahweh was quickly rewarded when she was taken into Pharaoh's palace as her own son's nurse. Jochebed was the first intercessor (mediator) for the deliverance of Israel. It wasn't only his birth mother who saved Moses. Shifra and Puah (the midwives) stood up to Pharaoh by saving the Hebrew baby. The motherly instincts of Pharaoh's daughter, too, saved him from destruction. There is meaning in every woman and all should bring meaning into their lives and those around them.

The list of significant women in the Bible goes on and on. There is the prostitute woman who found her way back through commitment. Others include Mary, a teenage Jewish girl, who became the earthly mother of Jesus. Other Marys include one of two sisters, who broke her best at the feet of Jesus. Mary of Martha shunned all customs and traditions as she found her way to the foot of her Lord. Her significant act of anointing the lamb is a testament to our intuition. Hannah faithfully returned her child, Samuel, to the house of God. We can't forget Ruth's tenacity and Naomi's graciousness. Manoah received instruction from the angel on how to raise a Nazirite, Samson. The Shunamite woman received her child back from the dead. The Syro-Phoenician woman dared to ask the Lord Jesus for the impossible, even though she was supposedly outside the covenant. Her faith brought healing to her daughter. Let's not forget Esther, the young girl whose words reverberate throughout generations, "If I perish, I perish," as she determined that salvation would come to the Jews through her willingness to become a significant vessel.

There are these in Scripture and many more living as heroes today. They are women who are not perfect, who stumble and yet rise again. These women lace the tapestry of our lives. They are unsung heroes who are hailed by their children. There are also mothers who have passed on to the other side, like mine, and still look down on their children. My powerful mother's influence is forever fixed in my heart. We are an army, intent and focused on the battle. Our armor must not fail us. We have been sent here for a reason, and we must rise up to take our places as the significant women of our generation.

6

Her Calling

The angel told Mary, Mother of Jesus,

> Hail, you highly favored
> The Lord is with you. (Luke 1:28)

Our ultimate example of a significant woman is Mary, the one who birthed, trained, and followed the Lord Jesus Christ. There is no higher calling than to be a mother, the channel through which God expresses His glory to this earth. Think about it! God could have directly created a world full of people, but He chose to replenish it through male and female. The female body, especially, became the instrument for God's deliverance, salvation, and abundance on the earth. The first woman, Eve, was deceived, because the enemy of her soul wanted to strip her of that crowning glory. We thank God that Mary got it right. Hallelujah!

Mother was designed to incubate and birth glory in due season. The first calling of woman was to dominate and replenish. This is a powerful calling, not to be taken lightly. We are positioned as vessels, hopefully fit for the Master's use. If we accomplish nothing else on earth than mothering our children, we will hear the ultimate acknowledgement, "Welcome, thou faithful and obedient servant."

As long as the woman understands the Great Calling delivered to her by the Almighty God, she will not be troubled by unnecessary and unrealistic standards.

> The man called his wife' name Eve [life spring], because she was the mother of all the living. (Genesis 3:20)

Eve's name, Life spring, is the metaphor of her calling. She will bring forth life. She was supposed to bring forth like her creator, but sin turned that around for us. The curse affected the delivery of the blessing, but didn't touch the blessing. Even in pain, we bring forth abundance.

> As soon as Zion was in labor, she brought forth her children. (Isaiah 66:8b) If you have been blessed with children, God has called you to be a mother.
>
> For we are God's workmanship, created in Christ Jesus to do good works, which God prepared in advance for us to do. (Ephesians 2:10)

To be a mother is to perform the duties of a mother—to conceive, give birth to, or raise and nurture a child. The word mother in Hebrew is *e´m*, "the bond of the family." We are the glue that holds it all together! Our position is that of power, not apathy.

My goal is to motivate all you mothers out there to rise up and take your position of power. Many of us know how to do this until our children become teenagers or young adults, when we become paralyzed by the onslaught of teenage demands. Some give up their power, while some become screaming generals. Either way, a significant mother is one who has stepped into her calling. God does not change His mind about our talents.

> For God's gifts and His call can never be withdrawn. (Romans 11:29)

He has called us to be His weapons on this earth. We are the gauges in the world around us. We are to be aware of what's going on with our children. A primary purpose might be to raise spiritual teenagers. Our words and behavior should constantly reflect our position of power. We are to keep speaking our children's future into existence even if their present behavior does not match what you're speaking. But we keep the words aligned to the scriptures.

> God then accepted the people He had already decided to choose, and He has shared His glory

> with them. What can we say about all this? If God is on our side, can anyone be against us? (Romans 8:30–31)

We have been called to this position of authority, which means that we are accepted by the divine. He will equip us for the job. God has never called anyone He didn't provide for. The ultimate question is what are you going to do with this call? Will you be distracted by the noise of a carnal society? Our goal is to accept and stand in this duty. We are to fight a winning battle. The apostle Paul encouraged the Corinthians to run to win! Our goal is to please the Master, and He wants us to become powerful mothers.

So let's briefly examine the definition of a good mother. Is a good mother one who stays home with the children? The one who works two jobs to keep a roof over her children's heads? Is it the one who stays in a loveless relationship so her children can have a father? Is a good mother the one who spends and slaves every moment of her day to accommodate the needs of her children? Her schedule is so cramped because she has to chaperone soccer, school field trips, music lessons, swimming, sleepovers, dances, and church activities. Most of us feel overworked and stressed. We are anxious for our children's future. We wish to protect and create better lives for them. We hold on tight to them when they are young and dread letting go when they are older. We pray over them night and day while in the throes of worry. Do all these make us good mothers? You bet! A good mother does what she can to the best of her ability. You can only walk in the light that you have. We cannot live better than our perceived truth. So, yes, a transcendent mother sacrifices for her children, but a godly mother lays them at the altar of God's love.

So we don't seek merely to be good mothers. We want to be significant even when raising our children.

QUALITIES OF A SIGNIFICANT MOTHER

Dunamis

Webster's dictionary defines *powerful* as someone who has great power, prestige, or influence. *Dunamis* (doo-nam-is) is a Greek word for force or miraculous power. It is used to describe power that reproduces itself. It is the Greek root of the word *dynamite*. This is the power that the disciples received in the book of Acts, Chapter 1. It is power from the Holy Spirit that empowers us to complete the ministry of cocreation. Dunamis is the same power that created heaven and the earth. It is the power that raised Lazarus from the dead. It is the power that gave Jesus the strength to endure the agony of the cross, ripped the grave open and freed him from the jaws of death. It is the infinite power present in creation. It is creative power. Dunamis power reveals truth and produces strength.

Dunamis is the power women everywhere need to raise their children. We can't do it alone. Women have been raising children since the beginning of time, but I would like to change your perspective on mothering. This book is about significant women. It is a divine calling, and when God calls you, He equips you. Dunamis is demonstrated when I know intuitively what's going on in my children's lives before they tell me, because I live in fellowship with the heavenly realm. It is waking up in the middle of the night to pray over my children, even though I don't understand the immediate need, or praying for a tender and loving heart toward a child who is acting up. It is anointing with oil when they're sick. Godly women learn to hear with spiritual ears.

Dunamis is passing on a legacy of passionate pursuit to a teenager who is wrestling with issues of peer pressure and personal beliefs. It is the ability to "let go and let God," when everything inside of you wants to dive in and rescue them from the consequences of their behavior. Dunamis knows that you are not alone. It is a total and complete reliance on the divine. Power is the ability to pray for my children's future spouses and friendships, starting at an early age. There is power inherent in our calling as women. We need to activate that power within every woman.

Prayer/Confession

> Lord, I ask for a renewal of your power in my life as a mother. Just as you called and anointed Mary to be the mother of the child Jesus, I ask you to anoint

me for this calling. I confess my inabilities and inadequacies. I confess I have tried to do this with my own strength. I exchange my inabilities for your power. I receive dunamis from heaven. I ask that the Holy Spirit continue to abide within me and lead me into all truth. I receive strength to run this mothering race to the finish. The mothering life is hectic, but I receive wisdom to do only those things You expect of me. When I am tired, Lord, lift me up and set my feet on higher ground. Thank You for Your grace. Thank You for loving me. I chose to be the powerful mother of my children today. Amen.

Prestige or Influence

The Brainy dictionary defines *prestige* as "the weight or influence derived from past success; expectation of future achievements founded on those already accomplished; force or charm derived from acknowledged character or reputation." In ancient Israel, the most important woman in the monarchy was generally the queen mother, not the queen. In the southern kingdom of Judah, the kings' wives were apparently never called "queens." It was the queen mother (Hebrew *gebira* or "Great Lady") who was honored and wielded authority as counselor to the king. Jeremiah 13:18 confirms the high position of the gebira in that she wears a crown (atara), like the king, as a sign of her dignity and position. The king and the gebira, identified as Jehoiachin and his mother, Nehushta (2 Kings 24:8), are seen as sharing a ceremonial moment on the throne, with Nehushta as co-regent.

Jesus's habit of meeting the needs of the women was a radical phenomenon. He was trying to change the old way of thinking about all women, not just the mothers of earthly kings. Jesus honored his mother at the Cana wedding by granting her wish. You see, the Jewish customs honored the gebiras of the time. These were the mothers of kings and royalty. It is no wonder that John's focus on Jesus as the "King of kings" elevated the status of his mother. He wanted to change the role of the ordinary woman to gebira.

I believe God wants to elevate the status of all women, even those who consider their jobs to be mundane or ordinary. You are royalty, and the children you mother are a chosen generation, a royal priesthood, heirs of the Father and joint-heirs with the Son. You bear in your body the sign of the creative power of divinity. Gebiras had influence on their sons, the kings, just like Mary got the attention of her son, Jesus. We also have the attention of the risen Son of God, Jesus Christ our Lord, because we are raising kings and queens for His kingdom. We are raising children who will possess the land for the king. We are women on a mission, and we have risen to the place of honor provided by God.

Prayer/Confession:

> I confess that I am a mother with influence, because I have the attention of the King of kings. I am

highly favored by God and give birth to destiny. I have favor with my children, even in their teenage and young adult life. I am a gebira in my house, and my children show respect. My children honor me, because I minister to their lives. I allow destiny to work through me for the purpose of mothering these children.

The Mystery of the Twenty-first Century Mother, or is it Maid?

I have seen slaves riding on horses and princes walking like slaves on the land. (Ecclesiastes 10:7)

I do not understand the twenty-first century mother who has become a caricature of the gebira mother. The caricature carries backpacks and books while the children walk beside her. She cooks and cleans the house and does laundry while the children play video games and engage in several extracurricular activities. She is the chef, chauffer, and maid. She is not respected because children do not value cheap labor. She is afforded no honor because she has lowered her status and they have no need for her opinions. The twenty-first century caricature believes that the world revolves around her children and therefore creates monsters instead of children. Monsters have no need for rules and regulations. They do not accept the principles of kindness and mercy, or justice and truth. They live a selfish existence because they have been taught to validate only their egos. When mothers rush to meet every need of the child, they stifle and create monsters. Let us examine a developmental theorist.

ERIK ERIKSON'S DEVELOPMENTAL STAGES

1. Infancy: Birth to eighteen Months

Ego Development Outcome: Trust vs. Mistrust
Basic strength: Drive and Hope

Successfully navigating this stage means that we have mothers who have persisted and met our needs. We will learn to trust that life is okay and develop hope and confidence. If, however, the mother or primary caretaker gave sporadic (undependable) care, then the child will grow up with issues of trust and learn mistrust because they were insecurely in their attachment.

Christian Perspective

The child should be nurtured from birth. There is a reason why women secrete milk during this stage—to nurse and nurture your child. The security of skin-to-skin love is the most secure feeling in the world, and your child will understand the love of God beginning from you. You are the gatekeepers. Begin to speak life-giving words to your children at this stage. As soon as they are born, it is important to "call" them into the world by naming them and blessing them. The child should be dedicated and blessings pronounced on him or her during the first forty days. This is an ancient tradition that allows the father or spiritual shepherd to pronounce a blessing on the child. If you are a single mother, it is important to find male mentors as soon as the child is born. Do not subscribe to a lie that you can do it all by yourself because you cannot. A child needs the wisdom of both parents to survive and thrive.

2. Early Childhood: Eighteen Months to Three Years

Ego Development Outcome: Autonomy vs. Shame
Basic Strengths: Self-control, Courage, and Will

During this stage, the child learns to master basic skills like talking, toilet training, walking, and feeding. This is when the child is learning right from wrong, gaining control over their body and learning to distinguish his/herself as an individual. The overbearing mother who shames the child during the building of these skills will wound the child's progress. The mother who does not allow the child to be an individual will also create low self-esteem and shame issues. At this stage, it is all right for the toddler to select outfits by themselves, choose between peas and carrots. All these will help develop a child with good self control, courage, and strong will.

Christian Perspective

This is the time to continue speaking wisdom and truth in to their lives. Begin to encourage your child so they can master any challenges and basic skills expected of them. The scriptures tell us that no challenge is unique but we all pass through the same. This tells your child that he too can be potty trained, he can make play selections. It also helps you as a mother keep your sanity because you have tapped into the grace of motherhood.

3. Play Age: Three to Five Years

Ego Development Outcome: Initiative vs. Guilt
Basic Strength: Purpose

Initiative is the most important skill learned during this stage. Your child will make up stories and role play or experiment with new ideas and concepts, like school, marriage, friendship, or what it means to be an adult. They begin to ask the why questions. If your child is stifled at this stage and does not get their questions answered, they may live with guilt.

Christian Perspective

Most importantly, I believe that this is the age that we should explain and actively demonstrate the concepts of Christ, like love, forgiveness, giving, receiving, sacrifice of sharing, and so on. Some parents do not want their children to watch the Disney fairy tales, but it encourages imagination. You can also introduce all the Christian tales like Veggie tales. My son loved the "Seven Brothers" when he was this age and we watched it a million times before it was finally buried.

4. School Age: Six to Twelve Years

Ego Development Outcome: Industry vs. Inferiority
Basic Strengths: Method and Competence

This is a very important stage that is sometimes not encouraged by parents, especially those who have to work two to three jobs to make ends meet. We have children who do not participate in extracurricular activities but spend hours socializing or watch television. Mothers who do not encourage their children to participate in community contribute to the development of an underclass. The child who participates on the debate team, community service, sports, and dance are developing latency, which means they are capable of learning, creating, and accomplishing numerous new skills and knowledge. This means they have developed a sense of industry. The child who does not learn to be industrious will develop feelings of inferiority and low self-esteem which could persist till adulthood.

Christian Perspective

Scripture declares that your child can do all things through Christ and for parents to "train up the child in the way they should go and he will not depart from it." It is important to train the child. The word *train* means "teach (a person or animal) a particular skill or type of behavior through practice and instruction over a period of time." Endeavor to teach your children the word of God. Let them memorize scriptures about who they are in Christ. Let them participate in extracurricular activities, including church and helping ministries. We want our children to develop a Christ-centered identity, not just a prepubescent personality.

5. Adolescence: Twelve to Eighteen Years

Ego Development Outcome: Identity vs. Role Confusion
Basic Strengths: Devotion and Fidelity

According to Erikson, up to this stage, development depended on what is done to us and, from this point on it depends on what we do. There is a need to develop an identity as preteens and teens struggle through social and familial issues that inundate them. My clinical students have discovered in the past year that the presenting problem with most teenagers is gender identity. These children have a sense of dissonance regarding their physical identity and sexual desires. There is so much children have to wrestle with during this stage. If their identity is not reconciled, the will become confused teenagers.

Christian Perspective

I believe that our youth are the future of any society. The kingdom of God was always advanced by the youth. David, Joseph, Esther, Mary, all were teenagers who realized their identity and road map very early. Joseph understood the transcendent principles of integrity and truth. David understood the transcendent principle of courage and strength. Esther served with fortitude and power of community. Mary understood faith and reverence. At this stage, the youth should be taught the transcendent kingdom principles of life.

The Transcendent Principles are:

1. **Faith***:* The ability to trust the unknown in order to effect change in the known. Faith knows that nothing is impossible and that there is substance all around you. Faith understands that you are in partnership with God and he will lead you as you follow.
2. **Love and Compassion:** Insight into the completeness of belonging to God and the family of faith. That you are accepted completely and totally in the class of the father, son, and Holy Spirit. We

must love the Lord with all our heart, soul, and mind while we love our neighbors as ourselves. This means that in the school of love, God is first, you are second, and others are last. It is important to love the Lord because it is from this relationship that the youth redefines his/her self concept. The acceptance of self leads to acceptance of others.

3. **Power and Authority:** The ability to comprehend that all powers belong to God, and as his delegation on earth, you have been endowed with an unalienable right of power and authority. This means that as a child of God, you can permit or disallow activities in this realm. We do not simply exist as mere men and women, when in actuality, we are representatives of God. What type of rep would you be if you had no authority or power to back your proclamations?
4. **Freedom and Truth:** "And you shall know the truth and the truth that you know will set you free." The youth in the kingdom is free from the limitations of the physical world and systems but first he or she must seek truth. Truth is the highest form of reality in existence. This means that no matter what subject or complex situation they are faced with, the youth must ask for the highest form available. Truth is God's way of thinking and doing. There is truth for sciences, arts, economy, family, religion, entertainment, media, medicine, politics,

and relationships. You are free once you discover the kingdom truths about these situations. No matter what you are being taught in the classroom, it is your reasonable service to seek the mind of God concerning knowledge. The Bible is not just literature, history, poetry, geography, science; it is the word of truth. Freedom without truth is short-lived. The youth is trained to look beyond the limitations because true freedom is a God-given right. The freedom to worship and serve the God of your choice, freedom to live authentically without influence from government or society, freedom to flourish and obey the will of God for all people for all time—use the resources of this world to serve God and man. The truth is that you have been sent to effect change in your generation and you now have the freedom to pursue your mission.

5. **Forgiveness and Peace:** Forgiveness is important if you want to maintain your peace. It is the ability to release the hurts of yesterday in order to enjoy the peace of today. The original Hebraic definition of *peace* is "nothing missing and nothing broken." Peace is not the absence of troubles, but the inward peace that is the guiding light of the believer. We teach the youth the Peace Decision Making Signals (PDMS). Green light is when you are sure in the mind and there is no anxiety or ambivalence. This

means you can proceed with the decision. The Red light is when you know that this is a wrong decision. The youth might be anxious, panicked, and fearful. These are all signs of the red light and you should not proceed. If you make decisions when your mind or spirit is conflicted, the end results will be unfavorable. The most confusing signal in this model is the Orange light. This is when you are unsure. You truly do not know which decisions to make or you could be ambivalent. We teach our youth not to make a decision with an Orange light. It might be that you need counsel or to gather more information, but decisions to proceed are only made at the Green light. The peace of God is that Green light that you rely upon.

6. **Justice and Righteousness:** Teach the youth to be just. Justice is not equality but equity—everyone gets what they need. Equality is implemented by governments, but equity is for my neighbor. We all might need the same things but at various times and in different amounts. Equity is that you allow your employee who has worked tirelessly the past few years to take an extra week off to mourn her husband even though she is out of sick leave. Equity is justice and our God is a God of justice and righteousness. Righteousness is making right decisions of fairness and ethics.

7. **Mercy and Grace:** Mercy is that I didn't get what I deserved while grace is that I received what I did not receive. The youth in this kingdom should reflect the principle in their actions and relationships. You extend mercy when you let someone off the hook for an offence or wrong done to you. Grace is when you give to fill a need or just because you are able to be a blessing.
8. **Destiny Work:** "You are God's masterpiece created for good works." This means that each youth has a purpose on this earth. I tell our youth that God has a designer's life prepared for them. On that path there is your spouse, career, and every one that is destined to help you. If you stray from this life, you will end up with loss, heartaches, and disillusionment. Don't let the excitement of youth cause you to forget your Creator. Honor him in your youth before you grow old and say, "Life is not pleasant anymore."
9. **Community:** Youth are taught that community of faith is important to their growth and edification but that the larger community is where they will make a difference. We teach them to expand their sphere of influence.
10. **Purity and Choices:** "Keep yourself pure." We teach the youth about making the choice to keep their bodies pure from fornication and sexual immorality. We have purity ceremony as a special celebration of this choice.

7

Three-Part Being

The powerful woman actively engages the tripartite being—that is, the spirit, soul, and body must be correctly aligned. The spirit must have preeminence over the soul and the body. The soul is made of up of the mind and emotions.

Your spirit connects you to the spiritual world and is the most authentic person. Your mind is the seat of your intellect, emotions, and decisions. Your body keeps you in contact with the world. Therefore, you are a spirit who has a mind (or soul) and lives in a physical body. If you believe that you are a spiritual being, you are better equipped for success because you have belief in something bigger than the appearance of your surroundings.

Your mind is the director of intelligence and controller of your individual life. It takes care of every requirement of the physical body without your conscious awareness. The mind has arranged the coordination of muscles, nerves, cells, and tissues. It relegates their repetition to the subconscious part of the mind. In addition to its subconscious functions, your mind also consists of your conscious emotions and thoughts.

The physical body is the basis of our experience in the world and life as we know it. It is the vehicle for movement, expression, and interaction with others.

The powerful mother consciously surrenders all three parts of her being to the goodness of God, so that she accesses the guidance, intelligence, and strength of God in serving her mission by using the following.

Faith

Faith sees with eternal eyes. It envisions what others cannot fathom. It visualizes you as a creative artist, even in the midst of a turbulent family dynamic. It sees you as a powerful preacher in the middle of your mess.

There is no other reality in this kingdom. Faced with the appearance of wayward, disobedient, and unruly children, you keep your calm assurance that "all is well and all will be well and all manner of things will be well." Your confidence is not based on what you see with your senses, because that is temporary (2 Corinthians 4:18). Temporal things are subject to change. We focus our gaze on eternal things, because they have the power to influence the temporary circumstances of this life. We hold fast to the bigger picture.

So when your family struggles to meet the basic necessities of life, or faces the loss of a child, sickness, or loneliness, you need to paint a heart picture of the truth. The truth is liberating. The things we see are facts, but they are not truth. Truth is unseen and eternal. The truth is what the word of God says about your situation. You are an overcomer. You can do everything through the grace of God. There is great power within you to counteract all evil forces that appear to affect your family.

Transformation happens from the inside out. We must see the truth within ourselves before it is projected out like a movie onto our lives. We are to command the revelation of truth to our circumstance. What else but faith could comprehend the fact that you will become a successful attorney, even though your mother was a drug addict, and you've never met your father? Who can fathom your being a powerful mother with spiritual children, when your mother was abusive or absent? Faith helps you venture out of your prison and dream bigger than your circumstances. You are a powerful woman when you dream bigger—for yourself as well as for your children.

Whatever and whomever you lay at the altar of God's grace, He'll return to you in better form. It is an uneven exchange—we exchange sadness for joy, pain for relief, inability for heavenly ability, and loneliness for friendship. Whatever you release to the kingdom will be transformed by God's mercy. Once we accept the things we cannot influence in the physical, we turn those situations over to God. How can you communicate with a teenager who refuses to talk with you? Certainly, there are skills that can be learned in communication, but there are some things that have to be dealt with in the spirit realm. When you quit yelling at your teenager and turn him over to God, God is able to overcome the rebellion that you cannot.

Significant women do not lie down and allow evil forces to take over their families, churches, or communities. We must become women that the devil has to contend with. Your jurisdiction must become a "no-fly zone" for all destructive and diabolical forces. Paul states clearly that,

> We are not fighting against humans. We are fighting against forces and authorities and against rulers of darkness and powers in the spiritual world. (Ephesians 6:12)

> We live in this world, but we don't act like its people or fight our battles with the weapons of this world. Instead, we use God's power that can destroy fortresses. (2 Corinthians 10:3, 4)

I remember the story of a mother whose son had rejected God and sought the darkness of the occult. He started wearing all black and worshiping the devil. Soon he moved away from home and literally joined the enemy. Before I continue this story, you must remember that we have a promise from God concerning our children.

> Teach your children right from wrong,and when they are grown they will still do right. (Proverbs 22:6, CEV)

You can hold fast to promise. If you have children who have moved away from the faith, expect God to make good on this promise! This is exactly what the parents of this demon-worshipping child did. For a long time, they did not know where he was, but they never stopped praying for him.

One day, they found out that he was on the streets of Los Angeles, California, living among drug addicts and other rebellious teens. His parents then made it a habit to take bags of food to all these teenagers and offer a word of prayer. There was resistance from the boy at first, but after a year of watching his parents feed and pray for him and all his friends, while helping anyone who needed help, he called home one night and asked to be picked up. This young man now helps others to get off the streets.

You have a promise from God that if you take the time to train up your children in the culture of the kingdom, they will grow to do right. It might take a while, but they will come back home.

Prayer

> Lord, I pray for my child, ____________*, who is involved in ____________ (name the activity). I have a promise from you that ____________ will come back, so I pray now that you bring him/her back. Thank you for loving and protecting ____________ while he/she is in this place. I pray that the light of God shines in ____________'s heart. Amen.

*Put your child's name in the blanks.

8

Her Body

> You're so beautiful, my darling, so beautiful, and your dove eyes are veiled By your hair as it flows and shimmers, like a flock of goats in the distance streaming down a hillside in the sunshine. Your smile is generous and full—expressive and strong and clean. Your lips are jewel red, your mouth elegant and inviting. (Song of Solomon)

Women should take care of their bodies because they are divinely crafted to be incubators and dispensers of life. From a biological standpoint, the goal of sex is to merge two sets of genetic information to create a human being that is genetically different from either parent. The product is a totally unique human being. Before the sperm and egg unite to create a baby, young women all over the planet experience the joy and pain of menstruation. This is when the woman's body starts to prepare for the great day of nesting. Women are life givers. It is time for us to step into our positions of privilege, instead of begging at the Master's gate. We have been called to bring life into this world.

> Yet you have made him a little lower than God (or heavenly beings) and you have crowned him with glory and honor. (Psalms 8:5)

Our position is powerful, so powerful that it almost got derailed with the first woman. I thank God that we, like Mary, can align ourselves to divine destiny. Mary offered this summation of her state:

> God took one good look at me, and look what happened. I am the most fortunate woman on earth! What God has done for me will never be forgotten. (Luke 1:48)

Since Jesus said he expects his followers to do greater things, then women must be a part of the "greater things" generation. God has taken a good look at us and called us worthy to be bearers of that treasure, realizing this brings us closer to the Father, the One who found us worthy to be used. We are not to boast in this. How many women know that children turn out differently than we expect? How many seek to be married while the biological clock is ticking away? We must still remain devoted instruments, fit for the master's work.

> We are like clay jars in which this treasure is stored. The real power comes from God and not from us. (2 Corinthians 4:7)

Our bodies are God's instruments for this purpose. He carefully crafted our bodies for the ultimate delivery of life. The powerful mother's body is a beauty to behold, both externally and internally. Her beauty has been blamed for the betrayal of men, but it is a perfect creation of God. King David set his eye on Bathsheba to the dishonor of his God and his power. Samson nursed at the breasts of Delilah to the loss of his anointing. King Solomon had his Queen of Sheba. We've heard of these, and of many modern-day ministries that had been toppled, because a "man of God" misused his authority over women. Men all through the ages have envied the power of creation and tried to possess it by possessing a woman's body. As the psalmist wrote,

> The greatness of the way I was made brings fear. (Psalms 139:14)

The crafting of the female body is deliberate and intricate. No one knows how much time the Creator spent fashioning the carrier of life. Eve was made as the crowning glory of God's creation. She was not an afterthought or accident. I believe that the Almighty stood back and waited for Adam to realize his need for a "life carrier." Adam was in awe of her beauty, but the real beauty was on the inside.

The brain is a woman's most sexual organ. The brain has the greatest influence on a woman's sexual response. This is one very good reason to hang on to your sanity, so you can enjoy intimacy with your Creator and your husband!

The primary function of a woman's breasts is to nourish her babies. The breasts are milk-producing glands necessary for the survival of her babies. Small muscle fibers cause the nipples to become erect when stimulated by cold temperature, breastfeeding, and sexual arousal. Research also indicates that milk composition changes according to the growth and healing needs of infants. The breast can never be truly "emptied" since milk production is a continuous process. We can never be "too empty" to nurture our children.[1]

Your body is the temple of God and was designed to bring human life onto this planet. You cannot become transcendent in the use of your design without knowledge of your instrument. Paul encourages the Romans to use their members as instruments of righteousness. Women are habitually using and misusing their members because of a lack of knowledge. I admonish you not to skip this section, but to get to know your external and internal reproductive parts. If nothing else, you might begin to enjoy sex with your spouse more.

Here is a quick study of your reproductive organs.[2]

The *vulva* is the collective name given to all your external sexual organs. The *labia majora* are the outer lips of the vulva. They consist of pads of fatty tissue and are sensitive to touch. Usually covered with pubic hair, they contain sweat and oil glands.

The *labia minora* are the inner lips of the vulva, which protect the clitoris, urethra, and vagina. They are inside the labia majora but have less fatty tissue padding. They are even more sensitive that the labia majora.

The *perineum* is the area of skin between the vagina and the anus. It is rich with nerve endings and is very sensitive. Stroking it can give great pleasure.

The *vagina* extends from the vaginal opening to the cervix. It contains lubricating glands that are triggered during arousal, intercourse, and orgasm. The vagina is also known as the birth canal.

The *urethra* is the opening that allows urine to flow from the body. It is not a sexual organ, but it is located beneath the clitoris and in front of the vagina. Because of its location, women can get bladder infections after intercourse if we don't practice good hygiene.

The *hymen* is a thin membrane that covers the opening of the vagina. It has a smaller opening that allows the release of menstrual fluids. The hymen is broken during the first sexual intercourse, and that can be painful for some women. It can also be broken with tampon use or some athletic activities, so a broken hymen does not mean that a woman isn't a virgin.

The *uterus* is the internal female reproductive organ that houses a child during pregnancy. It goes through cyclic changes and shedding of its lining every month. That is menses or your period. The uterus goes through rhythmic contractions during orgasm. The *cervix*, which is the opening located at the end of the uterus, is lifted during sexual intimacy.

The *clitoris* is a small area of spongy tissue that is rich in nerve endings. It becomes engorged with blood during arousal and orgasm. It is covered by a tissue called the *hood*, which retracts or pulls back during sex.

The so-called *G-spot* is a dime or half-dollar sized area that is extremely sensitive. It is located just beneath the front surface of the vagina, between the pubic bone and bladder. Some women report very heightened arousal if the vagina is stroked or pressed. For some women, there is immediate orgasm when the spot is touched.

The *ovaries* produce eggs for fertilization plus two hormones, estrogen and progesterone. If the penis hits an ovary during sex, it can be very painful, but this happens only rarely.

The *egg* carries one-half (twenty-three) of the chromosomes that make a baby. You can let this remind you that, as a powerful mother, you still don't have to carry the whole weight of Creation!

Estrogen signals an egg to begin ripening in the ovary. Estrogen also has an effect on breast growth. This is what aids breast growth during and after pregnancy. Some small-breasted women especially enjoy this aspect of pregnancy, because they actually venture into a C cup.

The *pituitary gland* produces the hormones FSH and LH. These hormones signal the ovaries to produce estrogen or progesterone, the two female hormones. It also signals the ovaries to function at puberty (when you begin having periods).

Progesterone signals the lining of the uterus, the endometrium, to change and become the nesting place for a fertilized egg.

The *thyroid gland* is the master gland of the body. It must be working properly, or your periods won't work like they're supposed to.

Why Say All That?

God is not afraid of the female body. He spent time crafting it. He designed it for creation, and he wants you to enjoy the process. Your internal organs are the key to your sexuality. The instinct to have sex is one of the most potent we possess. It's vital if we are to produce the next generation.

Apart from procreation, why else would I devote an entire chapter to sexual understanding? Mothers need awesome sex in order to maintain balance. Sexual arousal and orgasm involve interplay of several bodily systems. It's well known that sex improves our breathing and circulation, resulting in bright eyes, a facial glow, and shiny hair. Sex can also improve cardiovascular conditioning, strength, flexibility, and muscle tone. It even has been known to relieve symptoms of specific medical conditions, such as menstrual problems, osteoporosis, and arthritis.

Arousal and orgasm also benefit our mental health. Because they cause the release of pleasure-inducing endorphins in the brain, they can relieve anxiety and depression, increase vitality, and boost the immune system. Sex also creates an emotional and physical bond that is essential for social support. With all the mental and physical benefits of sex, it's like we're walking around with a complete health care system inside our own body![3]

Exercise is also very important for women because we are being pulled a thousand different ways. Some don't take care of their bodies and discover that they can't pursue passionate desires. Physical exercise of our musculature is essential to health and the continued vibrancy and vitality of our being. It is important to keep the body active. I am not talking about 24-7 at the gym. I don't believe that is necessary. It is not normal for the body to be all muscle. Just keep active. Get involved in something that is worthwhile to you. Just parking far away from the store can be part of daily exercise.

I love sweets! I mean, I can eat dessert for the entire day without any meals. I should rephrase that—I used to be able to exist, as a slim young woman, on ice cream and chocolate the entire day. But I can't do that anymore. Everything goes south. Before I know it, my butt is as big as a house, so I have to watch what I put into my body.

Don't get me wrong. I still struggle with choosing between healthy juices and ice cream. It's not such an easy choice for me. But if we don't feel good about our bodies as women, we will not be able to feel good about those around us. We either give them too little attention, or we go the opposite direction and hide our low self-image behind lavish displays of unhealthy attention.

Nutrition

Our bodies are vehicles through which God's vision is accomplished on the earth. Your vision or purpose dies with you if your body caves under the weight of maltreatment. The cemetery is filled with people who left behind unrealized dreams.

Second only to air in importance is water. Air is easily accessible to humans, because it covers the entire surface of the earth. Drinkable water can be found in abundant qualities in almost all parts of the earth. So drink as much water as possible. It will cleanse you inside, and you'll probably lose weight.

The eating of food, measured in the energy units called calories, is balanced by the work or energy released by movement of the body. If the intake of calories exceeds the outflow of energy, you gain weight. If the opposite, you lose weight. If we are sensitive to the needs of our body, we can more precisely determine which foods are going to provide our unique organism with the energies that are most conducive to its health.

This ultimately is a question for each individual, because there are many different diets that are effective in maintaining the various balances of the body.

Listen to your body. Take control of it. You are a spirit. The real you is not the physical body, so don't let its cravings take control of your life. Eat moderately, and that will be one less thing you have to worry about in your life.

The physical body begins to die from the moment it is born. Nothing conceived in the world of matter can achieve permanence. The body is only a machine, easily overtaxed beyond its capacity. Overworked and under-rested, the body pays the price. There is a balance for each of us. By being attuned to body, mind, and spirit, in harmony, one can maintain health and great awareness of many things, including bodily requirements.

The physical body is the means by which the spirit expresses itself. If it is overworked, it cannot fulfill its proper function. Sleep, for example, is necessary to bring refreshment and restore vitality to the physical body. Like nature, which prepares itself during the autumn for the sleep of winter, and then awakens during the spring to achieve the full glory of summer, our bodies must rest.

Present your bodies a living sacrifice, holy and acceptable to God as your reasonable service.

Prayer

Lord, I present my body a living sacrifice. I promise to honor and keep my body in good shape, eat well and exercise, learn to love and protect every part of this temple. The spirit of life radiates light inside of me, destroying any destructive cells and fighting attacking bacteria and viruses. I have good sex with my husband and I enjoy every minute of it.

9

Her Intercession

Hathach went back and reported to Esther what Mordecai had said. Then she instructed him to say to Mordecai, "All the king's officials and the people of the royal provinces know that for any man or woman who approaches the king in the inner court without being summoned the king has but one law: that he be put to death. The only exception to this is for the king to extend the gold scepter to him and spare his life. But thirty days have passed since I was called to go to the king."

When Esther's words were reported to Mordecai, he sent back this answer: "Do not think that because you are in the king's house you alone of all the Jews will escape. For if you remain silent at this time, relief and deliverance for the Jews will arise from another place, but you and your father's family will

> perish. And who knows but that you have come to royal position for such a time as this?"
>
> Then Esther sent this reply to Mordecai: "Go, gather together all the Jews who are in Susa, and fast for me. Do not eat or drink for three days, night or day. I and my maids will fast as you do. When this is done, I will go to the king, even though it is against the law. And if I perish, I perish." So Mordecai went away and carried out all of Esther's instructions. (Esther 4, NIV)

You Reside in the Palace with the King

The focus of this chapter is your location in the spirit realm. Esther's physical location was the palace, because she was married to King Xerxes. She was only allowed to see the king if she was summoned or scheduled. Now, here was her Uncle Mordecai, the one who had adopted and raised her in his own house, asking her to go beyond herself and step in to her destiny. Haman, the second in command to the king, had conceived a plan to destroy all the Jews in Xerxes's kingdom. Xerxes allowed Haman to kill them, but didn't know that his own wife was Jewish. Haman then gave the orders to kill the Jews, young, old, women, and little children on a single day, the thirteenth day of the twelfth month. When Mordecai heard about this, he went into mourning, tore off his clothes, and wept loudly at the palace gate. When Esther heard of the pain of her uncle, she sent clothes for Mordecai to replace the sackcloth he had on. When he refused to replace his clothes, Queen Esther sent her eunuch Hathach to find out what was bothering Mordecai.

Mordecai explained everything to Hathach, including the money Haman had promised to pay into the king's treasury for permission to kill the Jews. Mordecai gave him a copy of the order to show the queen and said that he wanted Esther to go into the king's presence and beg for mercy for her people.

Hathach went back and reported everything to Queen Esther. Her initial response was that going into the presence of the king was suicide. It was well known that if you went to the presence of the king without permission, you would be ordered to death. Mordecai, sensing her hesitation and fear, challenged the powerful spirit inside her.

> And who knows but that you have come to royal position for such a time as this?

Afterward, Queen Esther decided to obey Mordecai and plead for the Jews in the presence of this evil king.

> Then Esther sent this reply to Mordecai: "Go, gather together all the Jews who are in Susa, and fast for me. Do not eat or drink for three days, night or day. I and my maids will fast as you do. When this is done, I will go to the king, even though it is against the law. And if I perish, I perish." (Esther 4, NIV)

We are royalty in the kingdom of God. We dwell in a place of authority, and there are people at the gates crying out in silent or loud desperation, trying to catch our attention. We are sometimes limited, because of the prism through which we perceive our world. The silent cries of our children, spouses, extended family, neighbors, and city rise up to our ears through the person of the Holy Spirit. I believe Mordecai is an expression of the Holy Spirit. John 16:13 states:

> But when He, the Spirit of Truth comes, He will guide you into all the Truth [the whole, full Truth]. For He will not speak His own message [on His own authority]; but He will tell whatever He hears [from the Father; He will give the message that has been given to Him], and He will announce and declare to you the things that are to come [that will happen in the future].

We do not know how to pray, as we should. We are limited in our perception of events. Queen Esther was secure in her palace, while there was a death sentence on her people. All Jews were sentenced to death, and the most powerful Jew was in the palace!

Most of us are well-intentioned Christians. We attend our stained glass chapels, say our prayers, and try to live good lives while death surrounds us. We are happy to be Christians. Our belief systems tell us that we are not like the rest of "them." We don't commit abortion, adultery, or any of the other sins the church has exalted. (There is no hierarchy of sin. Gossip is just as heinous as abortion. In the presence of God, sin is sin). We live our modest lives in quiet contemplation, while the world around us is dying and aching. We are not aware of the plight of those around us, even our own children. We are not listening to the small voice of God within us, as He reveals the truth to us. Why is it that we are blindsided when things happen?

As women of authority, we have Mordecai within us too, telling us that we need to listen to the unspoken cries of our children. Some are under generational curses. They are becoming like that grandfather or grandmother who suffered depression or mental illness, or the great-grandfather who was locked up for murder. We have great-great-grandchildren of slaves still acting like slaves. There are generations of women on welfare or adulterers or whatever it is that seems to attach itself to the bloodline. You are sleeping with the enemy who happens to be your husband and he is addicted to porn. There could be assignments of evil in your office or home, and you just tune out, because it is easier not to talk about it or pay attention to it.

The Holy Spirit is grieved and trying to get our attention. What are you going to do about it, woman of God? What are you going to do about that teenager who is into drugs and fornication? What are you going to do with the evil that comes out of the mouth of your children?

What are you going to do about the abuse of your children? What are you going to do about a society that seems bent on taking our children to hell with them? What will you do when the lines between truth and sin are so blurred that we can't tell the difference? What will you do when your first grandchild is ripped out of the womb of your teenage daughter? What will you do when the perpetrator of evil resides in your house? What will you do when the minds of your children become callous with evil? What can you do when slavery mindset is operating in your house?

The Old Testament kings cried out to the prophet, asking for a word from the Lord. It wasn't that they were ignorant of God's words from times past, they simply wanted to know what God was saying about the present situation. The "logos" of God is the written word, while the "rhema" is the revealed and spoken word. We should always ask what the Lord is saying at this moment in our lives. This is why we need the Holy Spirit, who knows the heart of the Father and can reveal it to us.

What is He saying about your children? What is he saying about our jobs, neighbors, government, and even the world? Has He revealed any truths to you lately? A friend of mine told me about a time when her son was sick and miserable. They took care of him and stayed up with him all night. The husband later said God revealed to him that they should pray over his room. Well, they did just that, and the child was immediately better. Powerful women should not take things for granted. I'm not advocating chasing demons all the time, but we should realize that we reside in the palace. You might need to destroy the hold of the enemy on your children's minds and bring forth the blessings of God in their lives. Don't simply stop the strongholds of sickness, slavery, poverty, sickness, and death. Release the blessings of life, prosperity, health, and goodness into your children's lives.

A few days ago, I had a vision of a young boy walking around with chains on his ankle. However, he was not aware of it. I could see that the chain was affecting his walk, his talk, and everything he did. I also understood that the prism through which he saw the world was skewed. The surprising thing was that this boy was walking around as if nothing was wrong. I began to understand a lot about some of our black youth in this country. The chain represents the spirit of slavery that has attached itself from one generation to the other in one form or another. In the spirit of slavery, abuse has been perpetuated from one generation to the next. The spirit of slavery is kept alive by retelling stories and showing movies of yesteryears. It is sustained by systemic racisms and microagressions. We become what we see, hear, and say. Fortunately, as a child of God, you can stand on these promises of the Bible that release you and your children from generational curses. Let's fight for our children's future and sanity. This is a principle that impacts the next generation. Decide to become an intercessor today.

Christ redeemed us from that self-defeating, cursed life by absorbing it completely into himself. Do you remember the Scripture that says, "Cursed is everyone who hangs on a tree"? That is what happened when Jesus was nailed to the Cross: He became a curse, and at the same time dissolved the curse. (Galatians 3:13, The Message)

Therefore, there is now no condemnation for those who are in Christ Jesus, because through Christ Jesus the law of the Spirit of life set me free from the law of sin and death. (Romans 1:2, NIV)

For sin shall not be your master, because you are not under law, but under grace. (Romans 6:14)

And into the blessings of God:

My defense is of God, Who saves the upright in heart. (Psalms 7:10)

No king succeeds with a big army alone; no warrior wins by brute strength. (Psalm 33:16, Message)

So if the Son sets you free, you are free through and through. (John 8:32, The Message)

What are you, O mighty mountain? Before Zerubbabel you will become level ground. Then he will bring out the capstone to shouts of 'God bless it! God bless it!

> But on Mount Zion there shall be deliverance, And there shall be holiness;
>
> The house of Jacob shall possess their possessions. (Obadiah 1:17, NKJV)

Prayer/Confession

> Lord, I put an end to all generational curses that have attached themselves to my children. Jesus took our place on the cross, so we are redeemed from the curse of my ancestors. I remove the veil that is over the minds of my children and allow the light of truth to penetrate all darkness. Amen.

We are the brides of Christ. We have the attention of the Father, and our heritage is royalty. We need to make use of our position in Christ. Paul explained this to the Ephesians:

> And raised us up together, and made us sit together in the heavenly places in Christ Jesus. (Ephesians 2:6)

We are seated in heavenly places! Glory! So now what? What are we to do with our power and authority? We must do something. If we decide to remain in the status quo, and do nothing, we allow evil to prevail. Jesus asks a lot from those of us who have received his forgiveness and grace. If you are called by the name of Christ (Christian), then more is expected of you. A significant woman hears from God. She knows that to do nothing brings judgment and allows evil to prevail.

God commanded the children of Israel, through the prophet Isaiah, to "arise and shine." Jesus admonished us to shine our light and not keep it hidden. Mordecai's message to Queen Esther rings true to us today, "Become a mediator or an intercessor; speak for the voiceless, helpless and lonely, because this could be the reason why you were born." You, my friend, have come to the kingdom for a special reason. This is the reason you were born "woman." The privileges of motherhood come with certain responsibilities. One of those is to become an intercessor. Mordecai's mandate is for Esther to become an intercessor.

An intercessor is one who stands or bridges the gap for others. You will be the one to stop the attack of the devil in your household. You become the person who brings the presence of God to the situation. Powerful women are watchdogs in their homes. The devil cannot get a foot in, because you speak directly to the King of kings. I thank God for praying mothers, but an intercessor is more than a pray-er. She is sensitive to the ministry of the Holy Spirit. You go to God on the behalf of others. You pray until you receive your answer. Pray until something happens (PUSH).

> Likewise the Spirit also helps in our weaknesses. For we do not know what we should pray for as we ought, but the Spirit Himself makes intercession for us with groaning which cannot be uttered. (Romans 8:26)

An intercessor depends on the Holy Spirit to lead her in prayer. If you pray in tongues, this is the time to do so. Sometimes you simply have the urge to pray for someone but don't know the specific things to pray for. The Holy Spirit will help you pray. I believe that praying in tongues is a way to bypass your mind. If you don't believe in praying in tongues, ask yourself why it's so prevalent in other religions. We all know that the devil tries to counterfeit the things of the kingdom. Ask yourself why Hindus, Buddhists, and New Age practitioners chant mantras during meditation. You allow your spirit to take over your mind when you pray in tongues. Your human spirit is then linked with the Holy Spirit, who knows the specifics of the situation.

You have favor with God, because you choose to intercede for your children. Here are scriptural examples of women who interceded:

1) Esther interceded on the behalf of the Jews.
2) Anna, the prophetess in the book of Luke, heard the Holy Spirit and confirmed the arrival of the Messiah.
3) Abigail, the wife of foolish Nabal, who interceded on behalf of her family.

We'll take a minute here to examine the role of Abigail in the preservation of her family (1 Samuel 25). This event happened at a time when King Saul was out to kill David. He was jealous because God's hand was upon David's life, and people loved him more than Saul. David had taken refuge in the southernmost part of the country in the wilderness of Paran. His presence was a blessing to that land. It was good for the shepherds and farmers who constantly had to defend themselves from the raids of the Philistines. With David and his six hundred men there, the Philistines were somewhat more cautious.

Abigail and her husband Nabal were natives of that country. Nabal was an alcoholic, full of fear and ego. David could have said to Nabal, "Listen, I'm the future king of Israel. Give us what we deserve for what we've been doing in these days." Instead, he graciously had his men ask if they might have whatever Nabal could spare. But Nabal was indignant that David would ask for any of his hard-earned profits.

David was enraged when he heard of this and decided to teach Nabal a lesson by eliminating his family. When Abigail, the wife of Nabal, heard this, she sprung to action. She took two hundred loaves of bread, two leather bags full of wine, five cooked sheep, cooked grain, one hundred cakes of raisins, and two hundred cakes of pressed figs. She loaded up several donkeys and commanded her servants to go on while she followed. She did not tell her husband, because he was a foolish man.

She came face to face with David, the man who was to become king. She quickly got off her donkey, bowed her face to be ground, and began to intercede. She confessed the sin of her husband as if the error was hers. She praised David as the next king of Israel, all the while reminding him that killing a peasant would not reflect well on his future throne. She reminded him of the uniqueness of the God of Israel who was able to keep David's lineage in royalty.

Abigail's words struck a chord in the David's heart, and he granted her wish. This powerful woman singlehandedly saved her family from destruction. When she got home, her foolish husband was drunk, but she did not sit up feeling sorry for herself. She went straight to bed and got a good night's sleep. After Nabal died later, Abigail was married to King David.

That is the essence of intercession. You stand in the gap in order to protect a generation. You confess any sins they might have brought into the house and ask God to have mercy on your land. Your home is your land. Guard it jealously. Do not simply give up or complain and do nothing about the situation. There are some problems that can be solved in the physical or mental realm; others can only be solved in the spiritual realm. Some of our battles are in the spirit realm, and we must fight them there. Why intercede? Because God said so! Here are some scriptural references:

> And he saw that there was no man, and wondered that there was no intercessor: therefore his own arm brought salvation unto him; and his righteousness, it upheld him. (Isaiah 59:16)

For this cause we also, since the day we heard it, do not cease to pray and make request for you, that ye may be filled with the knowledge of his will in all spiritual wisdom and understanding, to walk worthily of the Lord unto all pleasing, bearing fruit in every good work, and increasing in the knowledge of God; strengthened with all power, according to the might of his glory, unto all patience and longsuffering with joy. (Colossians 1:9–11)

Epaphras, who is one of you, a servant of Christ Jesus, salute you, Always striving for you in his prayers, that ye may stand perfect and fully assured in all the will of God. (Colossians 4:12)

I exhort therefore, first of all, that supplication, prayers, intercessions, thanksgivings, be made for all men. (1 Timothy 2:1)

Confess therefore your sins one to another, and pray one for another, that ye may be healed. The supplication of a righteous man availeth much in its working. (James 5:15b)

And I sought for a man among them that should build up the wall and stand in the gap before me for the land, that I should not destroy it; but I found none. (Ezekiel 22:30)

10

Her Action

> I can already hear one of you agreeing by saying, "Sounds good. You take care of the faith department; I'll handle the works department." Not so fast. You can no more show me your works apart from your faith than I can show you my faith apart from my works. Faith and works, works and faith, fit together hand in glove. (James 2:18, The Message)

Transcendent women are not only to pray, they must also take appropriate action. You've heard the saying that, "Actions speak louder than words." So what should a powerful woman do?

Transcendent Women Protect the Promise

You must strive to protect what God has promised you at all costs. Remember that you are responsible for the promises God has given you.

Sarah, for example, put Ishmael out. The promise and the curse cannot live in the same house. You must uproot anything in your home that is not of God. Ishmael was the bastard child, the product of a union that was not blessed by God. Isaac was the child of promise. They both grew up in the same house for a season. There might be things going on in your house that you need to get rid of. God might allow the good and the bad to flourish together for a season, but there comes a time when God wants to clean house.

Sarah, the transcendent mother, sensed that the curse could not grow up with promise, so she told her husband to get rid of Ishmael and his mother. She got rid of the problem. She was a gebira. She had to guard her home jealously. Hers was a child of promise. He was set aside for the work of the Lord, and it was her duty to make sure that he grew up in a spiritual atmosphere. It was her duty to train him in the right way. Sarah cleaned house.

It is time for all transcendent women to clean their homes. Some of you already know what you're dealing with, while others have to ask God to reveal it to you. There are secrets in some families that are so dark they seem to stop the hands of God in our family. Remove the sin in the camp. The apostle Paul admonished the Corinthians, who were involved in all types of carnality, telling them that a small sprinkle of yeast finds its way through the bread dough. If your teenage daughter, son, or anyone else in your house is promiscuous, and you allow them to stay, what message are you passing along to the younger ones?

If the children of promise in your house watch you or your spouse act like hypocrites, you need to change. Getting the curse out of the house does not necessarily mean that you must kick someone out; it means that you should keep your house as a sanctuary for peace and holiness.

Our homes should be consecrated for the Lord, because we have children of promise living there. We should pray over the children to keep them safe, and pray over the house so no evil enters in. We are the gatekeepers of our homes. If there is anything that has become sin, idol, or immoral in your house, please get rid of it. For some of you, it might be as simple as limiting the amount of time your children spend listening to television and playing video games.

> Keep vigilant watch over your heart; that's where life starts. (Proverbs 4:23)

The heart is the core or center of a being. The heart is where life starts and flows from. In this verse from Proverbs, we are admonished to protect our hearts, for they are the genesis of life. Protect what comes into your home. Monitor what programs the children watch. Even some programs on Disney Channel are inappropriate. I still preview PG-13 movies before I allow my teenager to watch them. I don't think it's appropriate for a mother to allow children to watch sexually charged movies and videos. There is a world out there not concerned about the safety of your child's soul, so you must be concerned about it. How will your children ever hear the voice of God if their minds are cluttered with the things of the world? I believe that God is using children during this time, and it is our job as mothers to lead them to the throne of grace.

One of my happiest moments was when one of my daughters came up to me and asked to receive the gift of the Holy Spirit. I sat right there on the bed with her and explained what it meant to be baptized in the Holy Spirit. We prayed together, and my ten-year-old started speaking in tongues. Now, some of you might not believe in the tongue thing, but don't tune out the message, because the Lord is asking you to stand up for righteousness.

Transcendent Women Walk in the Spirit

The apostle Paul told us to walk in the spirit so as not to obey the dictates of the flesh. The best way to overcome fleshly or sinful desires is to do the things of God. Let your home become a house of prayer. Pray with your family. I am not talking about the nursery rhyme prayers of God bless me, my family, and I. I am talking about inviting the Holy Spirit to reside in your house. I am talking about taking authority over any demonic spirits that try to come against the work of God in your house. I am talking about exercising your rights as a believer, about approaching the throne of God boldly, about praising when you want to curse, about surrendering when you want to hold on, about crucifying your desires, about fasting and praying.

Allow others to see your growth in the Lord. Share testimonies of what God has done in your life. Share the love of God with others. All these things help create opportunities for your child to attain the promise.

How do you think Sarah felt when Abraham took their only son up to Mount Moriah to be offered up as sacrifice? Please don't tell me that she simply said, "Go in peace." I believe that Sarah also had faith in God, because He had kept his promise to her. He gave her Isaac after her own body had condemned her to childlessness. She knew that the God who was able to do that would not find it difficult to return Isaac back to her.

The other lesson is the impact of that experience on Isaac. This young Jewish boy must have been told the stories of his birth and how God had promised his father a seed. He was indeed the seed of promise. He carried within him the nations of the world. Isaac challenged his father on their way up to Mount Moriah. He said, "Father, we have the fire and the wood, but where is the lamb for sacrifice?"

Abraham's response demonstrated his faith. He said, "God will provide himself a lamb for sacrifice." At some point, Isaac must have known that he was the sacrificial lamb. He didn't struggle or try to run away. He had grown up with praying parents. He knew his mother was expecting him back home, and God wasn't going to disappoint her. He was laid on that altar, ready to be sacrificed to the God of his father. He then witnessed a miracle at that young age. He watched God substitute a ram for his life. He experienced the God of his parents that day.

Nothing can take the place of an experience. You own it forever. It was easier for Isaac to enter into promise, because he was raised in a godly home. Let us strive to make our homes godly for Christ. Provide your children the opportunities to experience God.

Powerful Mothers Give Their Children to the Lord

Just as Hannah, from the Old Testament, gave Samuel over to the Lord, we should turn our children over to God. It does not necessarily mean that our children will become priests or monks; it means we will release them to the Almighty Father. Hannah was one of two wives of Elkanah, a man devoted to God. Hannah pleaded with God to give her a son and also made a vow that, if she got her son, he would be dedicated to the Lord for the rest of his life and never cut his hair.

God had told the people of Israel that one of the ways to be dedicated to him was to become a Nazirite. Nazirites were people who made special promises not to cut their hair or drink alcohol. They gave their life to the Lord. This is a type of salvation, but for New Testament Christians, our salvation is not of the flesh. We don't have to go around with long hair, for it is not what we do that makes us Christians, it is who we are. Paul tried to explain this to the Galatians, who were trying to substitute salvation with the works of circumcision. We are saved by faith. Our circumcision is not of the flesh, but of the heart.

But faithfully, according to her beliefs, Hannah made a vow to dedicate this child to God. She finally received the promise of Samuel from God. God has given us a promise too, and sometimes our bodies fail to cooperate, like Hannah's. She was not only childless, but she also faced torment from her rival, Elkanah's second wife. Hannah was desperate to have children.

I remember that after I had a miscarriage, I immediately wanted to get pregnant again. The doctors advised that I wait at least six months, so my body could replenish itself. It was torture waiting those six months. I had to get pregnant again. I wanted what was lost.

So I can imagine being childless and craving the blessing of a child. Hannah craved Samuel with a passion, and she took action. She went to the temple to pray. She was in such deep conversation with God, that Eli, the priest, thought she was drunk. When challenged, she revealed her heart to the priest. She wanted a child desperately. She got her wish, but had to be willing to release her child to the Lord.

Hannah stayed home to nurse and train Samuel, and when he was old enough to eat solid food by himself, she took him to the priest and gave him back to the Lord. Samuel lived in the temple and later became the high priest and judge of Israel.

The first lesson we take from Hannah's example is to release our children to the Lord. The godly woman lays her children at the altar of God's mercy. If we would do that, we'd worry and stress a lot less, because we'd trust God enough to meet their needs. One night, while in my office writing, I started praising God. It must have been about 1:00 a.m., and the presence of God filled that room. One of the revelations that morning was a trust issue. God challenged me to completely place my trust in Him. When I remember the love of Jesus, how he went about doing good, I completely release things that I tend to hold on to.

Our children are not ours. They belong to the Lord. It is our job to lead them back to their Creator. Pray the prayer of salvation with your children. Worship together. Let them see Christ through you.

When we lay them at that altar of sacrifice like Abraham or leave them with the priest like Hannah, we are telling God that He has total control over these children. A friend once shared that her young adult daughter, who still lived at home, was living a wayward life. She would come home at any time she wanted and would be gone for days. My friend would stay up and worry about her, until one day, she got a "rhema" word from the Lord. "Do you trust that I've heard your prayers concerning your child? Do you trust me to take care of her?" That was the last time she ever worried about her child. There is no point in worrying about your children's future, if you turn them over to the Lord. God will take care of them.

Our children attended Christian private schools for a season. As a public school teacher, I had my reservations about public education. As parents of minority children, we felt private education was the best way to give our children the chance to succeed. We sacrificed to send them to Christian schools and were quite happy with our decision. Once our son finished sixth grade, we had to make a decision on the next school. Of course, we selected the best school around, which was thirty miles away from our house. It made sense to me, because he was getting quality education. My son was not happy at this school. He told me one day, "Mom, I have Christian friends. I attend a Christian school and live in a Christian home. When do I get a chance to actually witness to people my age?"

That didn't mean that one could not witness at a Christian school. It simply meant that God was telling me to let go of my tight rein on my son. It was a big decision to allow him to attend public school in the eighth grade, but it was a glorious one. He maintained his honors status, which is a great witness to his friends. He is not afraid to talk about Christ, and God uses him for His glory. I had to let go of my trepidations as his mother. I had to allow God to do His work in my son's life.

Release starts in the mind and manifests itself in the physical. The reason some of us are so stressed is because we try to help God out. We try to do our job, plus God's! There was no reason for me to be driving way across town to a school, when there were excellent schools down the street from us. Talk about added stress!

We need to let go and let God do His work in our children. It doesn't mean that we abdicate our responsibilities; it simply means that we get our priorities straight. Children are a gift from the Lord and should be given back to Him. Let Him inspire you to make right decisions. Leave them at the altar of grace.

11

Her Courage

Jochebed is one of the most powerful mothers in the Bible. I say this because your product is a good indication of your power. Jesus explained this concept in the gospel of Matthew 7, when he pointed out that we know the quality of a tree by the fruit it produces. Jochebed was the mother of Moses, Aaron, and Miriam. Imagine having children used mightily by God like these three!

Jochebed came from a lineage of priests. Her family was set aside to the Lord. She also became the wife of the priest Amram, and another family of faith was born. Jochebed's firstborn, Aaron, became Israel's first high priest (Exodus 30:30). Her daughter, Miriam, was a gifted poetess and musician who led the Israelite women in victory songs. Miriam assisted her brother Moses in delivering the Israelites from Egypt. Finally, there was Moses, a friend of

God and the great leader of the oppressed people of Israel, who led them toward the place of promise!

Before all these great acts of her children, Jochebed was a woman of faith. When she gave birth to her son, Moses, Pharaoh had just ordered that every son born to the Jews should be cast into the Nile River (Exodus 1). What would you do? This was a time of darkness and gloom. At times like this, we are called to be courageous. Jochebed had a relationship with the God of Israel. She was part of a family of faith. She knew that God had not blessed her with a son simply to take him away.

Some of you have children who are disabled. You know the agony of never seeing your child function like other healthy children. Others have been given a bad report of disease and death. What is a woman of faith to do? I call you a woman of faith, because you have the seed of faith in your heart.

God gave me a word of prophecy concerning each of my children when they were born, and I'm watching them live up to that prophecy, even though I have never shared it with them. Jochebed probably had similar prophecies or inclinations concerning her children. She knew there was something special about this child, Moses. God had a special plan for his life. She didn't sit there and cry and whine about what-ifs. She was a mother on a mission.

There is a time to pray and a time for action. Jochebed hid her baby from the wrath of Pharaoh. She defied the

king. It wasn't that she wasn't afraid, but she drowned her fears by springing to action.

James explained that faith without works is dead. You have to do something. If you live in a bad neighborhood with gang-infested schools, you are not being courageous by sending your children to school without help. If they have to attend that school, then become proactive. Take some initiative. Become an active participant in the school. If your child sees how serious you are about education, she/he will be too. Your most courageous act is to believe God to bless the work of your hands. Start a small business, and allow God to bless you to get out or change the neighborhood.

What is your act of courage? Is someone in your house abusing your children? Are you staying in an abusive relationship? What is your story of courage today? Every transcendent woman should be a walking testimony of faith and courage. If you lack courage, ask God to make you a courageous woman. The American Heritage Dictionary defines *courage* as "the state or quality of mind or spirit that enables one to face danger, fear, or vicissitudes with self-possession, confidence, and resolution; and bravery."

Jochebed demonstrated her faith in God by her actions. She created a basket fit for her son's safety. What are you creating in your family? Are you creating a basket of safety or a net of destruction? We have to examine the works of our hands. What atmosphere are we creating for our children? Are love, forgiveness, peace, and happiness in your home?

What are the big decisions you've made because a child or children were in danger? It takes courage to walk out of an abusive relationship. It takes courage to move your children out of the ghetto. Just like Jesus explained that we shall always have the poor with us, I believe that we will always have the ghettos, and you don't have to live there. It is easier for your child to become influenced by his environment than for him to change others. Is your act of courage volunteering in your neighborhood or moving across town? Ask, and God will direct you.

You have to give God something to bless. It is foolish to do nothing and ask God to move. Jochebed could have done nothing and lost the greatest leader Israel ever had. What are you willing to do to protect these children? It is an awesome responsibility.

I'm not only speaking to poor parents. God may have blessed you with material things, and now your children are the spoiled brats of this generation. They don't have limits and disrespect all authority, including yours. I was standing in the registration line, waiting to register one of my children for school, when I witnessed the most spineless act by a mother. Her daughter must have been a junior or senior in high school. Mother and daughter were waiting in line together. When it got to be their turn, the attendant asked them for something that was apparently left in the girl's car. The girl turned to her mother and berated her in front of everybody. "Mom, you are so stupid. I can't believe

you didn't do this, blah, blah, blah." This mother tried to placate the child, "Oh, baby, it's nothing. We can always go home and get it."

What is wrong with you, woman? I thought. This young girl did not start disrespecting her mother when she got to school that day. Young people always rise to your expectations. They are bombarded with examples in the media of children who disrespect their parents constantly, so you must be courageous enough to challenge that. I would have calmly told the girl that since she didn't know how to be respectful, then she didn't deserve to have a car. When the attitude changed, maybe in a couple of years, we could renegotiate the car. Do not let your teenagers walk all over you. You are the parent! It takes courage to be a parent in this society.

Don't become intimidated by the system. Don't be afraid to say no. Kids want you to become their maids, but let them to do things for themselves. We have become scared of everything. "What if they are kidnapped?" What if they are not? Do you want to raise children who are afraid to do things for themselves? The reason some women do so much for their grown kids is because they live in fear. Do something courageous today. Fear and courage cannot exist together.

Become like Jochebed, whose story did not end with making the basket. She set her baby's basket afloat among the reeds in the Nile River. She also sent her daughter,

Miriam, to keep watch. Jochebed knew that God would honor her courage. He always does! When the time came for the Pharaoh's daughter to discover the basket, Miriam negotiated with her to bring the baby home. Miriam, probably a teenager herself, stood boldly before royalty and conducted a business proposition. She offered to find a nurse for the infant, therefore arranging for her baby brother to go home and be nursed by his own mother.

What kind of teenager are you raising? Are you raising teenagers of honor or fools? It is not too late to begin the courageous acts of mothering. Courage has its rewards: Jochebed was paid for raising her own son when others were getting killed. Now that's a blessing.

12

Her Commitment

Higher purpose is the call to the mountaintop for all women. It means recognizing that there is something greater than us. Higher purpose is not individualistic. It is the plan of God for His people. We are heaven's representation on this earth, and our first assignment is to bring the kingdom of God to the world around us. Jesus taught his disciples to pray,

> Thy Kingdom come, thy will be done.

The kingdom of God here is not a physical entity but a spiritual one. We are spiritual mothers. Our citizenship is of heaven. We live in this world for a time, but our mission is from our heavenly home. As transcendent mothers, we must become committed to this way of thinking. Our first commitment is to the heavenly kingdom.

There are three types of commitments.

SPIRITUAL COMMITMENT

Spiritual commitments are powered by the dunamis power of the Holy Spirit. This type of commitment cannot be formed from your emotions. Spiritual commitments come from the still, quiet voice of God at the very center of your being, usually in the form of a revelation, or what I call an epiphany. Once your heart receives a revelation that transcends the mundane world's system, it requires an agreement on your part to transform the vision into a mission. Spiritual commitment requires you to see with "eternal eyes." Eternal eyes focus one's attention on spiritual truth. For example, if you spend time with God through prayer, reading the Bible, and receive revelation of His person, you will find out for yourself that He is not out to get you. You'll realize that the Great God of the universe is on your side.

Once you get that revelation in your spirit, you are obliged to agree with it and commit to the power behind that revelation. There can be no spiritual commitment without revelation. It is not enough to read the scriptures, attend church, and do "good works." Nothing can take the place of experience. You might be able to quote all the scriptures in the world, but if there has not been an encounter or revelation, you cannot have true spiritual commitment.

Spiritual commitment is what keeps you standing when everything around you is caving in. Spiritual commitment produces power during calamity. Spiritual commitment is not about being merely courageous, tenacious, or any of those good things. It is dynamo. It is power that reproduces itself. It is never lacking.

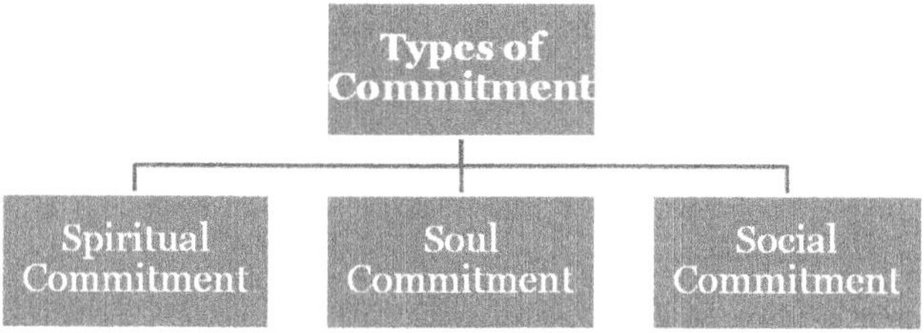

A woman with spiritual commitment can remain courageous while watching everything around her destroyed. Remember Naomi and Ruth (from the book of Ruth). These two women had lost almost everything, except for Naomi's earlier commitment to the God of Israel. Because of it, Ruth knew there was something about this God she didn't want to lose. They had both experienced God at some point in their lives. So when calamity came and Naomi was returning to the place of spiritual commitment, Ruth had no choice but to act. Ruth did not all of a sudden form a commitment when Naomi decided to return. What she did was simply voice her commitment to the God of Israel and reveal the action plan. Spiritual commitments will lead you to action. They are not complacent. If you know someone who complains about what's happening in their lives and nothing changes, they have not made a spiritual commitment. As transcendent women, we are called to spiritual commitments. Spiritual commitment looks upward.

> I will lift up my eyes to the hills
> Where does my help come from? (Psalm 121:1, NIV)

When we have a spiritual commitment, we are like computers connected to a network. We can download all we need at the appropriate time. Once you are committed to God's way of thinking, His ways of doing things, and His culture, then you have a connection with Him. God said that He is searching the earth, looking for someone whose heart is pointed toward Him to demonstrate His power. Can you believe that? This great Father is searching to bless us, but first he's looking for the connected (perfect) heart. The word *perfect* in the Bible refers to wholeness. He is looking for one who is wholly committed to Him.

This wholehearted love is right standing with God. He is seeking someone whose heart is committed or connected to Him, specifically so He can bless him/her. Why not you? Why not me? Why not all of us? Our heart's desire is to be linked up to the heavenly network, because we receive our programs from there. It is very easy to become a casualty of failed mothering without spiritual commitment.

As the gauge, you will be able to tap into the spiritual temperature of your children, or your office, or church, and so on. There are situations that need spiritual answers, but without a spiritual commitment, you will find yourself struggling to solve spiritual problems with earthly answers. Some of us have prayed—and are still praying—about situations regarding our children, and still there are no changes. One of the reasons could be that earthly solutions are not acceptable in the spiritual realm. You might have a child who is constantly depressed like you, and your mother or father before you, and you've exhausted all the medications and therapy to no avail. There is nothing wrong with medication when dealing with a medical issue, but it may be that spiritual forces are at work. You might need to break the hold of the devil on your child's mind.

You might need to intercede and fast for a time. There are so many diverse ways that healing takes place in the Bible, but how will you know which is specifically for you, unless you are connected to God? God wants us to bring His kingdom into our homes.

Mothers are spiritual connectors. They pray incessantly for their children. They anoint their children with oil. They take the Holy Communion at home. They speak blessings on their lives daily. They prophesy to their future, including future spouses and friends. They release the protection of God on their lives daily. They help them memorize scriptures. They pray. They dance. They worship.

They are happy together. If you're married, this ministry of training up your child is not only for your husband. You are the helpmate.

We should be able to touch the Father's heart. We should have access to the Father. We should be able to become mediators, even when we have the wayward child. If you have a child who has gone in the way of destruction, the spiritual connector in you will lead you to become a mediator. You will stand before God and ask for mercy. Cover him with the blood while they are out doing their own thing and follow the guidance of the peace within.

How Do I Become Spiritually Committed?

Create a space and a time for aloneness

Western societies sometimes shy away from separateness or aloneness. We are used to having church, families, and friends, but spiritual connection cannot come without solitude. We can experience God best in quiet places.

> After the earthquake fire, but GOD wasn't in the fire; and after the fire a gentle and quiet whisper. When Elijah heard the quiet voice, he muffled his face with his great cloak, went to the mouth of the cave, and stood there. A quiet voice asked, "So Elijah, now tell me, what are you doing here?"

We find the higher revelations of God in secret places. We need to find time to set ourselves apart to commitment.

You might need to write it in your planner. You might want to see it as a date with the Holy Spirit. To know Him, you must spend time with Him. Is it possible to know anyone without spending time with them? The reason some mothers have no clue what their children are thinking is because they don't spend time with them. You cannot know someone in a crowd.

If you only meet God in a crowd, He will always be just an acquaintance to you. Transcendent mothers are spiritually committed to an intimate relationship with God. There is no other way around it. Find the time and create the space. If the only quiet place is in your car or bathroom, then by all means feel free to hallow the name of God there. I love worship and interceding in my car. Sometimes I simply want to shout praises, so I get in my car to pick up my kids or run an errand, roll up my windows, and shout praises to His name. I turn off the radio and focus on the Spirit within.

Communicate

This sounds simple, but many people think that they don't have to talk to God, because he can read their minds. That may be true, but God has chosen language as a carrier of truth. Throughout Scripture, we are encouraged to ask, speak, say, shout—all having to do with our tongue. Can you imagine a relationship without communication? We communicate with God by speaking to Him. Tell Him what's on your heart. Remember the story of Hannah, the infertile woman who prayed daily in the temple. The high priest thought she was drunk, because she was speaking and nothing was coming out of her mouth (1 Samuel). Have you ever been at that place where all you can do is groan because the pain is too much? Tell God about your life. Let Him know the way you've been processing stuff. Talk to Him. Praise Him. Worship Him. If you don't have the words, open the Bible to the book of Psalms and read it out loud. Purchase the Bible on tape, and listen to preachers of the word. With practice, you will begin to know what to say. When you start this process, it will feel weird, but don't let that stop you. There is power in this seemingly small stuff. So talk to God about your children. Bring them to God, and leave them at the altar of His mercy.

Listen

In his sanctuary, there is glory, there is praise
In the presence of the father, there is grace and peace
I will come and worship,
I will listen and I will speak
Most amazing conversation
Most amazing revelation
As the God of all creation talks with me.

This paints a picture of our relationship with the Father. Communication is a two-way street. After you've talked to and worshipped Him, then you need to be quiet. Let God speak to your heart. It most likely will not be a thunderous voice. It will probably be a premonition or feeling that you have to move in a certain direction. He will speak to you primarily through His word, so it is important to study the Bible. But He will also speak to you through different vessels. Simply wait and listen for the leading of the Holy Spirit.

The Holy Spirit

God dwells in us through the person of the Holy Spirit. We have God on the inside. This is why John said,

> My dear children, you come from God and belong to God. You have already won a big victory over those false teachers, for the Spirit in you is far stronger than anything in the world. (1 John 4:4)

John told the church in the above scripture that the Spirit in them is able to withstand anything that comes against them. If you go back to Creation, you will find that the Spirit of God was moving over the face of the waters.

> The earth was barren, with no form of life; it was under a roaring ocean covered with darkness. But the Spirit of God was moving over the water.

God did not speak until after the Spirit had brought life to the earth. There is no darkness that can stand up against the Divine Spirit of Truth on the inside of us. Jesus called Him the Comforter. He is our Counselor, Helper, Advocate, Intercessor, Strengthener, and Standby. The reason we fear no evil, even when we walk through the valley of the shadow of death, is that we have this greater one on the inside of us. The powerful mother strives to understand this power.

Sometimes I feel that the Holy Spirit is just waiting for someone to acknowledge and allow Him to move. He is a gentleman who will not do anything unless He's invited. Why are we handling all the stuff of our lives alone when we have divine answers in our hearts? Why should your heart break over turmoil in your house when you have the Comforter residing within? Why should sickness and death destroy your children when the power that raised Jesus from the dead dwells inside you? The apostle Paul put it this way:

> And if the Spirit of Him Who raised up Jesus from the dead dwells in you, He Who raised up Christ Jesus from the dead will also restore to life your mortal bodies through His Spirit Who dwells in you. (Romans 8:11)

Acknowledge the Holy Spirit daily. Invite Him into your daily life. Benny Hinn's book, *Good Morning, Holy Spirit*, and Kathryn Kuhlman's autobiography, *Daughter of Destiny*, are excellent resources for understanding how to walk with the Holy Spirit.

I always try to recognize Him first when I get up from my bed. I ask Him for understanding of situations. Sometimes I don't need to check for the traffic update because I ask the Holy Spirit which freeway to take. God is interested in our mundane lives. His power is not just to perform miracles. Jesus said He will lead us to all truth. If there is any dark area of life that eludes us, the Holy Spirit will shine His light upon it, if we simply ask. The Holy Spirit does not force Himself into situations. He will watch you struggle until you invite Him in. He can help you locate that missing child. He can tell you what's going on with the child who has severed ties with you. Nothing will be hidden from you. He will teach us how to be powerful mothers!

I remember how one time my son sold his MP3 at school without informing us. He had just received a better one from us, so he thought he could dispose of the one he bought without our permission. Anyway, the person who bought it called the house, and I happened to pick up the phone. When my son later told me that he'd sold it, he was irritated that I already knew about it. I always tell my kids that they might as well tell me everything, because somehow the Holy Spirit will reveal it. We cannot do this parenting thing alone. We need a power greater than us. The power that was present in Adam to name all the plants and animals resides in us. We have the Holy Spirit as our partner. Welcome Him into all areas of your life today.

Prayer/Confession

> Holy Spirit, I invite You into my life today. I ask You to participate in raising my children. Lead and guide me into all truth that concerns their lives. Anoint me for this ministry of motherhood. Make me a woman of power. Thank you. Amen.

Action

Often we say things like, "Well, I'll try. I guess I could. I hope I can." That's not commitment. Commitment is simply two words, totaling five letters: Commitment is *I will.* It's that simple. Commitment is *I will.* My struggles and experiences over the years have proven to me that commitment gets the job done. That's what separates the achievers from the sustainers.

> My meat [fulfillment] is to do the will of Him that sent me and to finish His work. (John 4:34)

As believers, our first commitment is always to the Lord.

> I do always those things that please the Father. (John 8:29)

The book of James encourages us to demonstrate our faith by the works we do. You must do something with the truth received from the divine source that dwells within you. The act of aligning your thoughts with truth will be examined in the section titled "Soul Commitments." The spiritual realm is an action realm.

Jesus told his disciples in Acts 1:8 that the result of abiding with the Holy Spirit is power. We've already talked about dunamis earlier. It is energizing, creative, sustaining, and stimulating power. Powerful mothers will tap into this power in order to obtain promises. Life is a series of low and high roads. We can only learn to navigate successfully by the power of this divine being. If the Bible says to pray, then we should pray. If it says we should worship God, then we should do that. "Train up the child in the way of the Lord" is a biblical commandment.

If we are citizens of a higher place, then we need to learn the language and culture of that country. We are ambassadors to this world, and our children are our responsibility. How can we represent the kingdom as true ambassadors if we have no revelation of truth about our land? Powerful mothers learn the culture of heaven. They learn to speak the language. They speak for the kingdom and bring the kingdom to their children.

Commitment hears the heart of the Father. It helps us find our area of anointing and stay with it. It knows without a shadow of a doubt that you are a part of the intricate will of God, which would not be complete without you. We are created for a higher purpose. How many would like to accomplish the things that have been revealed in their hearts? I believe this is the time for spiritual commitments for God's women. Women were the last of His creation for a purpose. They are His finishing touch, the crowning glory of His creation. He wants to show us off to the world like never before, as we commit to His kingdom.

SOUL COMMITMENT

Why is it that some people are successful, while others never seem to achieve much? What's the secret that pushes some of us over the top, while others never even begin the climb? There are many reasons—low self-esteem, a negative attitude, and non-belief, to name a few. But the largest obstacle between higher purpose and us is a lack of soul commitment.

Soul commitment means committing to the total transformation of the mind. It involved replacing failed paradigms with winning ones. Spiritual commitments are formed in the spirit. Soul commitments carry out the details orchestrated by the spirit. Paul told the Romans (in the twelfth chapter of the Roman epistle) who had already made the spiritual commitment to renew their minds (Chapter 12), that he wanted them to be complete.

You see, when you became a Christian, your spirit was renewed and your intentions were good, but the mind remained the same. This is why you find yourself still craving some of the unhealthy stuff of the past. Our souls, or minds, must be renewed in order to impact our world effectively. We are to examine our thoughts and mind habits in the light of kingdom thoughts, so we can then correct any discrepancies.

Commitment is a dynamic force that all human beings possess. How many of us work with someone who constantly complains about her workload, swears she'll never take on another project, and then does? She may say she's committed to balancing her life, but she's more committed to her old identity as the hardest-working camper. Until she allows that old identity to die, and her true self to be resurrected, then she'll continue to overcommit and overextend. Our actions demonstrate our commitment. Commitment is not what we say, it's what we do.

Soul commitment begins an adventure. It is the backbone and driving force of achievement. Commitment is the triumph of possibility over all the reasons why "it can't be done," of creation over mere change. Commitment and the power of your word set new worlds into motion.

Examples of Negative Past Commitments

- Staying in abusive situations
- Allowing others to walk all over us
- Never allowing anyone to get close
- Distrust of authority
- Being better than
- Never taking a vacation
- Being right
- Proving society is biased

- Never becoming happy
- Intimacy problems

Past Soul Commitments

Soul commitments dictate the events that we allow into our lives. Commitment emanates from the deeper recesses of our soul realm and demands action. Whether you know it or not, everyone is honoring past commitments. You may have inherited them, or decided on them even before you were eight years old. Commitments can be as basic as "I must eat to protect myself, because my mother starved herself to the point of hospitalization," or "I must please my father," especially if he was hard to please. We make subconscious commitments not to get close to people, because we've experienced a loss and think we can't bear to face that again.

We are all honoring commitments from our past. Most commitments that rule our lives were made during our developing years. They may have helped us make it through, but these commitments get in our way now. They are thoughts we formed while watching our parents, society, and environments. They were experiences we had no control over.

It's natural to live our life from the soul realm. It usually takes a conscious effort and divine intervention to focus on the spiritual realm. The soul realm dictates most of our actions. The problem with that is we are spiritual beings with spiritual commitments, so we have a war transpiring between our spirits and souls. The apostle Paul stated in Romans 7:21–23 (The Message):

> It happens so regularly that it's predictable. The moment I decide to do good, sin is there to trip me up. I truly delight in God's commands, but it's pretty obvious that not all of me join in that delight. Parts of me covertly rebel, and just when I least expect it, they take charge.
>
> I've tried everything and nothing helps. I'm at the end of my rope. Is there no one who can do anything for me? Isn't that the real question?

In other words, we are set in our ways before we accept God's grace. The culture of heaven is different from our mind's culture. The mind has taken digital photos of everything that's ever happened to us and formed commitments that dictate our lives.

If you have a behavior pattern that you can't seem to break, it could be because there are commitments that need to be altered. For example, if you're afraid of abandonment, you will find yourself constantly sabotaging relationships no matter how much you crave one. Your commitment to the fear of abandonment is far greater than your desire for a healthy relationship. If your daughter experiences abuse in your home, either physical or emotional, she will either make a commitment that love is abusive or never to be like her weak mother. Either way, she will spend the rest of her life running away from her mother or running to the same type of abusive relationships. This paradigm that was formed as a child will have been transferred to the subconscious mind by the time she's old enough to start dating. She notices a dangerous pattern, and she knows that she wants to change, but can't seem to help herself. Even when she knows what the Scripture says, she can't seem to break the pattern.

Imagine the little girl in this example is now married to husband number two. She is thirty-five years old and has two girls of her own, who have watched her repeat the cycle of abuse. She has a spiritual awakening and becomes a child of the kingdom. She attends church regularly and volunteers for every possible committee, but she still struggles with this mind issue. Why? The process of soul commitment can only be achieved by personal assent. God cannot renew our minds without our participation—it is our duty. I believe that the reason Jesus had disciples was to help them in the transforming of their lives. He wanted to show them a new way of living.

How do we change past commitments?

Acknowledgement

Ask that the Holy Spirit, the divine being on the inside, reveal the truth about your situation. If you are involved in negative patterns and don't understand why, ask the

Holy Spirit for illumination. He will bring things to your remembrance. Even with a simple prayer like "God, I am willing to understand why I act this way. Holy Spirit, reveal this to me, in Jesus' name." You don't have to struggle to remember, it will come to you in time. Your subconscious is already working on it, because your attention is now centered on that particular area. There may be some things you might not want to remember, so a general acknowledgement of willingness is desired.

Prayer/Confession:

> Lord, I need your strength in releasing my past commitments to you. I lay them down at the cross now. I do not want any part of the ugliness of my old nature. I am a child of this kingdom, and I choose the power of this kingdom over the prison of my past. Release me from the pain and hurts of the past. I receive power to continue this process of transformation.

Grief

Grieving over the past might be the next step for some. It could mean that our thirty-five-year-old example has to mourn the loss of her childhood and her innocence. She was denied a peaceful and happy home. Some women have been raped and abused, abandoned and left alone, used and mutilated. It's appropriate to grieve those things. They were never God's will for you. Even Jesus wept, right before he resurrected Lazarus.

Release

In our example, the thirty-five-year-old lady now understands that those past commitments have to be severed. She has acknowledged the problem of the past, asked God to heal that little child, and grieved her wounds. Now she is free to let those wounds go, along with all the behaviors attached to them. Releasing the hold of past soul commitments is like spring cleaning before we bring out the spring furniture and fashions. Jesus reminded the people of his time that they could not pour new wine into old wineskins. New wine expands and will burst through the old skin. The same goes for this process of transformation. Release comes in the form of consciously letting go of the past, weeping over losses, writing letters, keeping journals, screaming for a while, the list goes on. Don't overlook professional help or support groups! As Paul's letter to the Romans indicates, we can't fix ourselves alone. By the time you get to this phase, you will hear the Spirit guide you to the right help for you.

Restoration

> The LORD is my shepherd; I shall not be in want. He makes me lie down in green pastures; he leads me beside quiet waters, he restores my soul. (Psalms 23: 1–3a, NIV)

Your inner healing is not complete until God restores your soul. He will release you into your destiny. Restoration is a phase of replenishment. You will be given strength for your life's journey. Just like God promised to restores Job's diseased body to that of a young child (Job 33:25), so also God restores our soul back to its original state of beauty. He gives us a second chance to trust again. He opens the prison door to the soul and allows us to walk into light. Some souls are worn out from years of war. There is no muscle for forgiveness or release. Dejection, depression, and disease have settled in. You need power greater than your own to release you from the prison of heartache and sinking sand. You seek one day, or just one moment, of sanity. You long just to think clearly again, to smile, cry, and run. You crave the loving touch of a mother or father. You seek the girl who was abandoned. Today is your day of restoration.

Most of our commitments are formed during our developing years. This means that most human beings spend the rest of their lives honoring commitments formed because of the actions of other people—daddy, mommy, sister, brother, other relatives. The only thing that can change a prior commitment is a higher commitment. Thank God for new birth! The Bible states in 2 Corinthians 5:17:

If any man be in Christ, he is a new creature, behold old things have passed away and all things have become new!

Prayer/Confession

> Lord, I need you to help me. I am sinking deep into the quicksand of my negative thoughts. I am so far from where I want to be. I am troubled and cast down greatly. My soul is in mourning for all the wrongs that have been inflicted upon me or that I've inflicted upon others and myself. I cry to you under the burden of my soul. I am a broken woman. Deliver me from this place of gloom. Restore my soul back to me. Free me from the bondage of my own lies and the quagmire they made of my soul. Like the psalmist, I cry out for restoration. Jesus, set me free. You promised that your freedom is the only lasting grace (John 8:36). I love you. Thank you for this freedom. Amen.

Our commitment now is to a higher being, to the God who created us, the King of kings and Lord of lords, the One who captures the essence of salvation in the resurrection of His only son. Our commitment should reflect the heart of the Father. We know that commitments have consequences in the realm of action. If we are committed to the Father, our actions will manifest His will and purposes. Commitment to the Father will break down the walls of our hearts as we spend time in His presence. If we are committed to somebody, we want to please that person and spend time in His presence. Only when God touches us can we see His greatness and understand our own smallness. Only then can we see things His way and gain the power to live by a higher standard than our own.

Mary, Sister to Martha and Lazarus

The other Mary is that sister you hear the preachers extol. She was the perfect sister, the one most of us love from a distance. I've come to know Mary these past weeks. She represents what can be achieved when we commit to seeking the heart of the Father. Mary is at the feet of Jesus all three times we meet her. She achieved her greatest work in John 12. Mary, because she had spent time with Jesus, was promoted. Commitment will promote you. She listened to his words and spent time with the master.

Later on, days before his death, Mary was the only one who got it! She understood that her master and friend would soon be put to death. Even though Jesus had talked to his disciples about his dying, they didn't seem to grasp the urgency of the moment. But this woman got it. The significance was lost to everyone at that table but the Master and Mary.

Therefore, she received strength to carry out her mission. She defied all tradition by making herself known in the presence of men. Imagine if you will, Mary pulling back her chair ever so gently, rising with her box of alabaster in her hands. All eyes are on Mary now. She has taken the first step, and every single nerve in her body is screaming for her to sit down. She feels Martha beckoning her to sit and not embarrass the family. Lazarus is intently focused on his sister, who is taking the Master's attention off of him. She could deal with the stares of the disciples, but as Mary moves closer to Jesus, her heart yells out to all the forces trying to control her.

> There is a reason why I can't turn back now. You see, I remember those painful nights before He walked into my life. I am aware of the shame of not having a husband and the agony of losing my brother, the sole provider in the household. You see, Martha, I spent time with Rabbi Jesus, because I was going crazy. My world was falling apart. I needed someone to lift me out of the sinking sand. It wasn't that I didn't want to serve with you, Martha; it was that my commitment to Him had consequences in the realm of action. I apologize for embarrassing you, but my face is set like flint. I have to anoint his feet and worship one last time. You see, he's sitting right there, the Ancient of Days revealed for a short time. What I am about to do pales in comparison to what I've received from him.

So Mary once again found herself at the Master's feet. She uncovered the box of expensive perfume and poured it on his feet. The whole house was enveloped in her love for the Master. As she untied her hair (another break from tradition) to wipe the master's feet, Mary completed her greatest act.

As Jesus staggered through the streets of Jerusalem, with the hatred of men unleashed at him and as drops of blood paved the road to Calvary, Mary's perfume rose up as a sweet smelling savor. Every time he caught a whiff of that perfume, he remembered Mary's commitment, and it warmed his heart to keep moving in the direction of the cross.

So there we have the tales of two women—the first received anointing to birth the Anointed One, while the other anointed Him for his death journey. These two women were committed to their higher purpose, so they achieved their greatest work. They saw the kingdom of God manifested in their lives. They stripped themselves of self-consciousness and self-confidence, which are enemies of commitment.

My prayer is that we renew our commitment to the Father. God's higher purpose is for His women to manifest the desires of His heart. Let us take a minute to pray that each day finds us closer to the Father. It is only when we draw close to Him that we receive dunamis to perform His will. Whatever yoke seems to bind us or prevents us from being committed to Him, we break it now in the Name of Jesus.

Prayer

> Lord, I yield myself to your higher purpose. Let me find my purpose in you. As I spend time with you, reveal your will to my heart.

SOCIAL COMMITMENTS

Since the family is not an isolated system, we find ourselves making commitments to the social structures around us. There are commitments to schools, jobs, friends, churches, and more. Sometimes, our social commitments are a direct result of our inability to say no to others or our skewed belief in perfection. A mother's social commitments stem from soul commitments. If your soul has been restored as I shared in the second section, then your spirit and soul are in sync. When this happens, it becomes really easy to navigate social commitments. You will begin to filter all your social commitments through a narrow prism of truth. If it doesn't line up with the mother's higher purpose, then it may not be the season for it. So you will not commit to the PTA after school, for example, when you've made a commitment to tutor your child in math after school. Take time to filter your social commitments. Remove and add engagements as the seasons of your life change.

Write Your Commitment

> Write the vision, and make it plain upon the tables, That he may run that readeth it.For the vision is yet for an appointed time. But at the end it shall speak and not lie. (Habakkus 2:2–3)

Now, when our innermost desire finds its satisfaction in God, we will not be racing around for other thrills. We will not be driven by money, career, success, or public opinion. We will have no other gods before God. Everything else will be brought into subordination to God. The commitments we make to our families will flow from our desire to honor God and do what He says. The commitments we make to the church will be made in that framework, in obedience and worship of God. The financial commitments we make will serve God, and not mammon. Life will have a stable order and structure to it, because it will have the right foundation.

We need to write our commitments. The most effective way to begin your journey as a powerful mother is to put your commitments in writing. You should write a Mother's Statement of Purpose. A clear vision of your purpose will propel you to action. You will become purpose driven. It doesn't matter if you are twenty or forty years old, a clearly written purpose gives you direction. Consider why you feel so passionate about your purpose, vision, or dreams as a mother. The statement of purpose is one of the best ways that you can demonstrate your spiritual, mental, and physical development, ability to think clearly, and knowledge of your purpose. It should be important enough for you to want to know exactly what you're getting into, and that you have the commitment to survive.

My challenge is for you to stop hiding in the shadow of success. Break out of the shell of missed opportunities and misconceptions. The whole world is waiting for you to shine God's light from within you. Life's urgent question is "What are you doing to make your world a better place?" There is no better time than *now* to start planning your life. Dare to reveal God's good will to the world around you. This book is designed to help you change your thought process. It is designed to assist you in discovering your intrinsic desire for success, not in the eyes of the world, but in the eyes of God.

> Shine, for goodness sakes, and stop hiding behind a smokescreen of self-doubt, ignorance, and self-pity. It's your life, don't mess it up! (Akin Merino)[1]

Living Commitment Profile

I **spend** most of my time **doing:**

____

____

____

____

____

I **spend** most of my time **thinking** about:

____

____

____

____

____

I **spend** most of my extra **cash** on:

I **spend** most of my time **talking** about:

I **spend** most of my time **listening** to:

I am **consumed/obsessed/passionate** with/about:

Based upon these expenditures, my commitment is to:

____

____

____

____

____

Mother's Statement of Purpose

What is purpose? Encarta defines it as:
Noun (plural pur·pos·es)

i. Reason for existence: the reason for which something exists or for which it has been done or made
   - the purpose of life
ii. Desired effect: the goal or intended outcome of something
   - the purpose of the law is to control pollution.
iii. Determination: the desire or the resolve necessary to accomplish a goal
   - you need to act with purpose.

Transitive verb
Set something as goal: to intend or determine to do something
pur.pose.ful [púrpəssfəl]

1. Determined: showing a clear determination
    - she set off with a purposeful stride.
2. having a goal: having a definite purpose or aim
    - purposeful activity

Writing your Mother's Statement of Purpose (MSP) shows a clear determination to achieve optimum success in this calling. What could be more important than fulfilling one's purpose? What could be worse than living in the shadow of success for the rest of your life? What is your purpose? What is your reason for being here on earth? What is the purpose of this high calling?

You begin the journey of excellence by writing down the vision. You might not become a Mother Theresa, but you will certainly become a powerful force in your home. Your purpose could be to bring peace to your confused children, to teach math to teenagers, to beautify your home, or to find a cure for the common cold. Whatever the Holy Spirit has revealed to you is your purpose.

What you should know about purpose:

1. Purpose doesn't have to be ostentatious or showy, but it must be resolute.
2. Purpose doesn't have to be grandiose or extravagant, but it must be significant.

Complete the following statements based on the truths in your life regarding motherhood. Think about dreams and visions you have for yourself and your children. Remember the things that get you confused or sad. What are you passionate about? Most of these will change as you grow older, but you need to start with what you have.

Remember, you are making declarative statements about yourself. Do not take this part lightly. It is your first step to success.

1. My name is ______________________________
2. I feel ______________________________
3. I am a ______________________________
4. My dream is to ______________________________
5. I see myself ______________________________
6. I am confused ______________________________
7. I am annoyed when ______________________________
8. I am happy ______________________________
9. I am sad ______________________________
10. I wish ______________________________

11. My Miracle life ______________________________

____

____

12. My Statement of Purpose is ______________________________

____

____

____

____

- My purpose is to create peace and goodwill in my family.
- My destiny is to be the best mother that I can be, in whatever situation I find myself.
- My purpose is to help create an atmosphere for God to move in my life and that of our children.
- My destiny is to allow God to rescue my family from the generational curses of poverty, sickness, and bitterness, and to allow the fruits of God's blessings to flow through me to my family.
- My destiny is to use laughter as a healing balm in my home.
- My miracle life is to have love and acceptance from my family, a city of refuge ministry.

13

Her Private Victories

When you have committed your life—spirit, soul, and body—to the will of God, you will become successful, because you have laid the foundation for a successful life. My definitions of success are posted on my office wall—"Success is living a significant life."

We cannot live significant lives if we are encumbered by what I have termed the 3Ds: disruption, distraction, and distress. A mnemonic device is to think of disruptions as distractions that cause you distress. If you don't have money to pay your electricity bill, how can you live a significant life? How can you live a significant life if you are distressed over real financial difficulties, family issues, career and educational problems? You cannot become a success until you fight your way out of life's 3Ds. Disruptions are life's roadblocks—poverty, sickness, death, divorce, separation, loss. Distractions are frustrations—false accusations; broken friendships, annoying habits. Distress is an internal state. It is the impact of the disruptions and distractions. If you have been making loud noises at your roadblocks or praying for the roadblock to open up and it still remains blocked, binding the devil, praying and fasting against this roadblock and it still remain blocked, it might be time to find the detour. The scriptures say there is always a way of escape, a landing place. Take time away and seek new solutions because there is substance all around you. There is always an answer to your problem, but it might not be where you've been focusing your attention. Disruptions can be a diabolical means of keeping you from significance. Apostle Paul admonishes us to rejoice in all situations not because we are suffering but that there is a way of escape. No matter what you might be going through at this moment, remember that there is a way of escape. Your case is not closed unless you close it. It is not over unless you determine that it is over. There is nothing impossible for God, and he has determined to give you a landing place. The solution to disruption is another way of seeing, doing, thinking. Basically, you need a paradigm shift. Most people keep trying to fit a square peg into a round hole. If you're having problem attaining any of your goals, get assistance, learn new skills, and strive to exit the rut of disruption.

Distractions are irritants or frustrations that are best overcome by self determination and inner strength. You make a decision to demonstrate love and forgiveness. Learn to eat and exercise right so that you are not so easily flustered.

Distress manifests or activates a dormant mood disorder called major depression. According to the National Institute of Mental Health, symptoms of depression may include the following:

- difficulty concentrating, remembering details, and making decisions
- fatigue and decreased energy
- feelings of guilt, worthlessness, and/or helplessness
- feelings of hopelessness and/or pessimism
- insomnia, early-morning wakefulness, or excessive sleeping
- irritability, restlessness
- loss of interest in activities or hobbies once pleasurable, including sex
- overeating or appetite loss
- persistent aches or pains, headaches, cramps, or digestive problems that do not ease even with treatment
- persistent sad, anxious, or "empty" feelings
- thoughts of suicide, suicide attempts

Warning signs of suicide with depression include:

- a sudden switch from being very sad to being very calm or appearing to be happy
- always talking or thinking about death
- clinical depression (deep sadness, loss of interest, trouble sleeping and eating) that gets worse
- having a "death wish," tempting fate by taking risks that could lead to death, like driving through red lights
- losing interest in things one used to care about
- making comments about being hopeless, helpless, or worthless
- putting affairs in order, tying up loose ends, changing a will
- saying things like "It would be better if I wasn't here" or "I want out"
- talking about suicide (killing one's self)

In the faith–based community, we must treat the depression with a three-tier approach—spiritual, medically, and organically. I discussed this in my book *Soul Desires: Restorative Tools for a Woman's Spirit, Soul and Body.*

14

Her Successes

Proverbs 31:10–31 is what success looks like!

A good woman is hard to find, and worth far more than diamonds. Her husband trusts her without reserve, and never has reason to regret it. Never spiteful, she treats him generously all her life long. She shops around for the best yarns and cottons, and enjoys knitting and sewing.

She's like a trading ship that sails to faraway places and brings back exotic surprises. She's up before dawn, preparing breakfast for her family and organizing her day. She looks over a field and buys it, then, with money she's put aside, plants a garden.

First thing in the morning, she dresses for work, rolls up her sleeves, eager to get started. She senses the worth of her work, and is in no hurry to call it quits for the day. She's skilled in the crafts of home and hearth, diligent in homemaking. She's quick to assist anyone in need, reaches out to help the poor. She doesn't worry about her family when it snows; their winter clothes are all mended and ready to wear. She makes her own clothing and dresses in colorful linens and silks.

Her husband is greatly respected when he deliberates with the city fathers. She designs gowns and sells them, brings the sweaters she knits to the dress shops. Her clothes are well made and elegant, and she always faces tomorrow with a smile.

When she speaks, she has something worthwhile to say, and she always says it kindly. She keeps an eye on everyone in her household, and keeps them all busy and productive. Her children respect and bless her. Her husband joins in with words of praise: "Many women have done wonderful things, but you've outclassed them all!" Charm can mislead and beauty soon fades. The woman to be admired and praised is the woman who lives in the fear of GOD. Give her everything she deserves! Festoon her life with praises!

Every mother needs to experience personal success.

Human beings are created for success. Once you accept the possibility of succeeding within your world, the rest becomes easy. Jesus said, "It is done unto you as you believe." It's not what you want, it's what you believe that counts. Believing in the possibility of your success changes your life. Your conversations will be different. You behave differently, and even dress differently as you pursue your goals. Your nature rejects failure. Its greatest cry is to rise above adversity and mediocrity. If you would just follow that inner desire, you will become a winner.

A successful person is someone who is aligned with her destiny. Successful people are "in tune" with their winning nature. Nobody is born a loser. We all begin life with everything we need to succeed. You already have within you all of the ingredients you need to rise above your circumstances. Failure is not an option. Live your desires!

Mothers often settle for not achieving their goals in life for a myriad of reasons, even though becoming successful and fulfilling those dreams is easier than they probably think. Mothers are sometimes our own worst enemies. When it comes time to commit to the fulfillment of God's dream for our lives, following our passions, or achieving our ambitions, we often manage to talk ourselves out of doing what we'd really love to do.

Some mothers try to live vicariously through their children. Others put their dreams on hold, waiting for some unknown future day to start living them. The rest make the best of things and just decide they weren't meant for anything greater than their current lot in life.

Don't get me wrong. You know I believe being a transcendent mother is definitely an achievement to be proud of. But there are a lot of you who love being mothers, but who also feel a hunger stirring in your spirit for something more. Don't let anyone tell you there's anything wrong with that, because there isn't. Remember the Proverbs 31 woman!

Many mothers talk themselves out of going further in life—maybe because they're afraid, or maybe because too many people told them they couldn't. Maybe they feel they'll be selfish to their families. But the truth is that the best gift you can give to your children is a powerful mother who follows her dreams and makes them happen. It teaches your children, especially your daughters, to follow their dreams and trust God for their fulfillment.

That's why I want to give you the tools you need to break free of the status quo, achieve your full potential, and fulfill your dreams in life.

The first thing you need to do is set some goals for yourself. Goals are action steps that support your purpose. Trying to be successful without clear goals is like trying to find a destination without actually knowing where you're going. You might circle around the same spot for hours, and then give up and go back, never realizing that you've arrived where you wanted to go all along.

There are a few things you need to know about goals in order to set them successfully. First, you need to set two types of goals: long-term and short-term. Long-term goals should be things you hope to achieve in a year or two, or even longer. These are your big ambitions in life, the things you want to achieve but have been too scared to try. Short-term goals, on the other hand, should be things you can complete in a week, in a month, in three months, and so on. Each short-term goal, ideally, will take you one step closer to achieving your long-term goal.

Second, goals need to be specific and concrete. That means you have to avoid goals such as “I want to be successful,” or “I want to be a powerful mother.” How are you going to determine when you’ve achieved those goals? You can’t. Specific goals should be things like “I want to start my own business,” or “I want to make time to take my family on a vacation this year.”

When I say your goals should be concrete, I mean they should be observable items you can write down. When you don’t write down your goals, you either settle for less as you go along, or you forget about them altogether. That’s just not going to work. Buy a journal, or have a file on your computer, where you can write out your goals. Let no one else read them, unless you want them to. Each time you achieve a goal, cross it off the list and add a new one. Every time you see how much you’ve accomplished, you’ll feel even more motivated to keep going.

Third, you have to reward yourself for the goals you meet. Just because you’re an adult doesn’t mean you shouldn’t treat yourself when you do a good job. Think of some things you’d love to do but usually don’t. You might buy yourself a treat, spend a day at the spa, splurge on Godiva chocolate, take a day off from work to watch soap operas, go to the movies, lay in bed all day with a good book, or best of all, celebrate with friends.

Each time you cross a goal off your list, you need to reward yourself. It helps fix the miracle of your accomplishment in your mind. This helps you when you need encouragement in the future. It's also a powerful way to encourage others to meet their goals.

Once you've set some goals for yourself and have begun to achieve them, you may find that the higher you climb toward your ultimate goal, the more nervous and anxious you become. That might surprise you. You may have thought that each success would make you feel more and more comfortable. The truth is, it works just the opposite.

You see, each of us have our comfort zones. Our comfort zone includes where we live, who we know, what we do, and how we live. Each time we achieve one of our goals, we are taking a step beyond our comfort zone. This causes our body to feel anxious, because we're entering unexplored territory. That's where our fear comes from, the unknown.

As we keep going further outside of our comfort zone, we increase the chances that fear will overcome our desire. There is, however, a way to combat this problem. It's called visualization.

What most people don't realize is that they can trick their own minds. You simply close your eyes and picture yourself doing something successfully and comfortably. You see yourself, your picture the surroundings, you feel the positive feelings associated with your achievement. Afterward, your brain will believe it really happened, and you won't be afraid, because that activity or event is no longer unknown to you.

It really works. Athletes, musicians, actors, politicians, and others use visualization to improve their performance. Picture yourself successfully achieving your next goal as soon as you complete one goal. Instead of running back to hide in your comfort zone, you are actually moving your comfort zone so that it includes that next goal. Instead of being bound by your limits, you're stretching them!

As you progressively climb this ladder of goals, you may be surprised by the reactions you get from some people, particularly the people closest to you. One woman I know works at a business college where she meets lots of young women who are trying to fulfill educational goals in their lives. One thing she hears from many of them is that their husbands, children, parents, friends, and even bosses aren't supportive of their decision to return to school. That lack of support sometimes causes them to drop out of school before they earn a degree.

You'll face the same types of reactions from people as you start trying to achieve your own goals. They may hide their negativity by complaining that you never have time for them, or they may be blunt and say that you'll never get where you are going. Don't hate them for their reactions. They can't help it. You see, as you are stretching your comfort zone, you also stretch theirs. They might worry about losing you because of the changes you are making in your life. Instead of dealing with their insecurities, most people try to get you to change back so they won't have to change. It's just human nature.

You can understand it, but you don't have to let it stop you. You can ignore their complaints or their negativity. You can confront them about their fear of change. You may even separate yourself temporarily from some of the more negative people in your life. Don't worry. Those people are usually not your children. Children tend to respect and admire their mothers when they try to make positive improvements in their lives; adults are often less appreciative.

The bottom line is that you have to do whatever is necessary to prevent them from bringing you down. Remember, their comfort isn't worth sacrificing your dream or your hard work, no matter who they are. It's good for them when you shake things up every once in a while!

There's one more thing you can start doing now to help yourself feel and become more successful—*act* successful. Our perceptions and feelings aren't static. They are impressed by our actions. Think about a time when you've been sad or worried, then watched a funny movie on television. When the movie was over, and you had laughed and smiled for a couple of hours, you were in a good mood again, because that's how you were acting.

Another example is illness. When we act sick, we feel sicker. When we start moving around and stop thinking about feeling bad, we forget about being sick.

It works with success too. The more you act as if you are successful, the more convinced your mind will be that you are already a success. As a result, you'll have improved self-image and self-confidence, which will help you achieve your goals even faster. The more goals you achieve, the more successful you'll feel. Before you know it, you've created a positive cycle that will catapult you directly to that long-term goal, ambition, or passion you want to fulfill.

A Living Purpose

Purpose is the reason for existence, and discovery of your purpose is an exciting process. Everything has a purpose. The purpose of time is to give us a measure of eternity. The purpose of your house key is to grant access to the house. What is your purpose as a woman? What will you achieve? Purpose could mean doing more than you've ever done or doing something differently. Purpose demands action.

You are living your purpose at this moment in your life. The only problem is that you might not know the big picture. We are always anticipating something greater and different from our present situation. We dream of a better spouse, house, career, or car. We want to be transported to the place of perfection. The good news is that there is always a better tomorrow and a higher purpose for your life. The reality of our lives is that today matters!

We are in this moment because of the choices we have made. Those choices, whether right or wrong, will lead us to the greater tomorrow. Even if this current reality is not what you want or planned for, it is your reality. Unless we learn to accept the reality of today, we cannot embrace tomorrow's purpose. When we surrender today unto God, He will use all that has come before to serve His higher purpose for your life.

15

Her Education

Since mothers often put the needs of their loved ones before their own, I want to explain why you should further your education, both for yourself and for your family.

So often, you put your own passions and desires on hold so you can help the rest of your family fulfill their own dreams and ambitions. The truth is, however, you are doing them and yourself a disservice if you don't follow your heart, use your talents, and pursue those talents to their full extent. Remember Jesus's parable of the talents? God gave you your talents and dreams to serve His higher purpose!

You know by now that I'm not suggesting that you should abandon your family. What am I telling you is that there are ways—ways you may not have considered—for you to achieve your goals while also caring for your family. I'm talking about furthering your education.

Right now, all of you transcendent women are at different stops along your educational journey. A few of you already have advanced degrees, while some of you have not yet gotten your high school diploma. No matter where you are now, you can go further.

Before I give you some specifics, let me address the question: “Why? Why should I go back to school? How would this help my family? What’s the point?” Well, I’ll tell you.

There are three main reasons why you, transcendent mother, should go back to school. The first reason is that you’ll become a powerful role model for your children. You want them to go as far in their education as possible, because you know that in today’s world higher education has become synonymous with higher levels of success. But it’s easy to tell kids what they should do while we do the exact opposite. When you pursue your education, you are showing your children just how important it really is.

The second reason is that you’ll be prepared for a career or mission. Even if you are a stay-at-home mother right now, that may not be your future. We can’t predict everything that will happen to us, and we all have to prepare for the worst, even though we are hoping for the best. If something happened to the breadwinner of your family—illness, unemployment, disability, etc.—what would you do to support your children? What kind of job could you honestly acquire with your current level of education?

Would you actually be earning enough money to keep a roof over their heads, food on the table, and clothes on their backs? Furthering your education will help you provide for your children no matter what happens.

Many of you may have had bad educational experiences in the past. Some of you may be ashamed because you haven't graduated from high school. You may even think you aren't smart enough to get a diploma. Don't let those negative feelings and experiences keep you from doing something you know you want and need to do. You aren't unintelligent, and you shouldn't be embarrassed about decisions you made in the past. What matters is your future. And in your future, you can finish high school by taking your GED. GED stands for General Equivalency Exam. It's a test of the same basic subjects you'd cover in high school. It's administered locally so you don't have to travel. There are no classes to take, but you can find books that will help you prepare for the exam at your local library. The best part is that the GED exam will open the door for better employment and higher education for you. The best way to get started, if you're interested, is to visit the American Council on Education's web site at www.acenet.edu or contact the school board in your city.

After you have that GED, a diploma, or even if you have some college experience, you can take your education even further. I know mothers don't have time for traditional college classes, and many of you worry that you wouldn't fit in with the eighteen-year-olds anyway. The alternative is online education. You can go to bible school online.

No matter what level of education you currently have, you'll be able to find an online program that will match your needs and your ambitions. An online education has many benefits over the traditional brick-and-mortar colleges. You can work at your own pace, you have convenient access to instructors by phone or email, you don't have to leave your home, you don't have to plan a class schedule around your family's commitments, and you won't have to sit in class for hours. I truly believe that online college programs are one of the best gifts technology has given us.

Education is one of the greatest gifts you can give yourself and this world if that's what you need for this next level of your life. It's an investment in you, your potential, and in the future of your entire family

16

Her Business

Mothers, whether they work at home or away from home, can find personal and professional fulfillment by starting their own businesses. It's easier than most people realize. According to the Small Business Association, a woman owns one of every three small businesses. Those are impressive numbers. Only a few decades ago, women's roles in the work world were limited to secretaries, nurses, and teachers. What I want to talk about is not how or why that transformation has happened, but how you can become a part of it.

There are several good reasons to start your own business. Working mothers can spend more time with their children because they have more flexible work schedules. In many cases, they can even work at home so that they can be there when their children arrive from school. It's also easier to attend school or family functions. Stay-at-home mothers find ways to channel their passions into something that serves a higher purpose, even beyond their children's lives. It also allows them to contribute to the family income and improve their standard of living, without the feelings of guilt they might experience working outside of the home.

If you like the sound of those possibilities, then consider starting your own business. Of course, it isn't easy. It requires commitment and perseverance, like the rest of your mothering ministry.

I'm going to explain some of what you need to know in order to start a business, but I won't be able to cover every detail you'll need. My advice is to visit the Small Business Administration's web site to get more detailed information. The SBA's Women's Business Center discusses financing options, shows you how to create a business plan, and teaches you about marketing. You can find them at www.sba.gov.

What I want to address here are some of the things you need to get your business off the ground. One of the most important is to decide what type of service or product you are going to provide. All of us have some talent, interest, or passion that could be turned into a business. For example, as powerful mothers, you know a great deal about raising children, so you could channel that knowledge into your business. You may create products to help children stay safe, provide tutoring services, or train babysitters. Those are just three ideas out of hundreds of possibilities. The important thing about making this choice is to pick something you love. If you don't, then running your own business won't be any more enjoyable than having a nine-to-five job. In fact, it might be worse, because it will require more of your energy and input.

You also need to determine whether there is a market for your product or service. That's not hard to do. The next time you find yourself with other mothers at the park, at your children's school, or at a birthday party, just casually ask around. Mention the idea and see the reaction you get. You'll be able to tell how much interest there is in what you want to offer.

The next step is to determine how much money you need to get started. If you plan to work from home, you'll have to make sure that your office is equipped with the necessities: telephone, computer, and appropriate workspace. Once your business starts to grow, you may find the need to expand, which can be extremely exciting, but it's better to start small and have big expectations than to start big and be disappointed by the results.

Most businesses today, including the majority of small businesses, have a website. Having a presence on the Internet is going to be a great way for you to gain clients because it's affordable and reaches millions of people all around the world. To set up a website, you'll need three things: a domain name, hosting space, and a web designer.

Domain names are website addresses. For example, sba.gov is a domain name. You'll want to pick a domain name that refers to your business, either by name, acronym, or product/service. Otherwise, it will be too difficult for clients to remember. The domain name will cost you around $20 to register for the entire year, and you'll have to renew it every year.

Hosting space is also easy to acquire. The space is the physical location of your website. When someone enters your website's address into their Internet browser, the address will point to that location and allow visitors to view your site. You generally rent your space on a monthly or yearly basis. The costs vary, but you could expect to pay as little as $10 to $20 per month. You'll want to shop around until you find a hosting service that you feel comfortable with and that provides a guarantee on its service.

Finally, you'll need to hire a web designer. Of course, you may be fortunate enough to have family members, even children, who can create websites. In that case, you should definitely use their services to help you. Otherwise, search your local yellow pages and call around. You may be able to find local talent at an affordable price. By affordable I mean less than $30 an hour. Hourly prices vary dramatically from one designer to another, so it's worth it to shop around.

You also might want to post your need at elance.com or guru.com, where it is free for you, as the buyer, to post a project. Then, you can receive bids from web designers and see if any of them feels right to you. If that doesn't pan out for you, call your local high school or technical college. Explain your needs, and ask for any students who have the necessary skills and would like to gain some professional experience. Chances are, they'll be able to recommend someone to you.

To help your web designer, be clear on what you want for your site. You may want to browse through other sites to find design elements that you like and want to incorporate so that you can give them specific examples to work with. Of course, if you don't want to have a website right away, you can choose from a wide variety of other marketing methods, such as distributing flyers, sending out letters, or partnering with another small business. Have an open mind and think of any possible way that you could reach potential customers. Get estimates on the cost of the advertising and include those expenses as you plan how much money you are going to need to start your business.

While we're on the subject of money, this is a good time to bring up a couple of other excellent reasons to start your own business. One is that it will provide you with an abundance of tax write-offs. Everything that you use for business purposes can be claimed on your taxes and can help reduce your tax payments at the end of the year. When I say everything, I mean it! If you have a separate office in your home for your business, you can claim parts of your mortgage payments and your utility bills as business expenses. If you use your car to buy stamps or purchase office supplies, then you can deduct the mileage and the gas you used during the trip. Of course, you'll need to keep track of all of these things, but it will be worth it in the end.

Another good reason is that you can give your children some experience in real-life working situations. Mothers of teenagers can put them to work answering phones, filing, or running errands. Younger children can help with stapling, organizing, and filing. Giving your children something to do as part of your business will show them that you trust them and see them as responsible individuals. It will also make your business more of a family affair and will allow you to spend some quality time with your family. It's also a good idea to pay your children for their help, perhaps hourly. You should have them keep track of the hours they worked and what they did, both to teach them responsibility and to give you a record for tax reasons. All the money you pay them can also be deducted from your taxes.

I hope you realize that this is something you can achieve, if you feel drawn to do it. Unlike nine-to-five jobs, starting a business, particularly a home-based business, can bring your family closer together and can be a meaningful and rewarding experience for all of you.

17

Her Rejuvenation

Transcendent mothers need to recognize the importance of taking vacations. Even God took Sunday, remember? When I talk to mothers about their passions, one statement almost always comes up: "I wish I could take a vacation!" Working mothers, stay-at-home mothers, mothers of teenagers, mothers of young children, all of them tell me that they'd love the chance to relax without the responsibilities of the home or of work. The bad news is that fewer of them, and of Americans in general, are fulfilling that need. In 2003, 12 percent of all workers made no vacation plans while even more took less time than they had previously. Furthermore, 40 percent of Americans say they don't have enough time to relax. A significant portion of people claim not to have *any* relaxation time. You probably fall into one of those two categories.

What's most distressing about this trend is that you're not getting the chance to experience the many benefits that vacations can deliver. Let's look at some of those benefits, so you can see why it's so important for you and your family to take vacations.

One benefit is that vacationing allows you to broaden your horizons. If you always stay in the same city or same general area for most of your life, then you're missing out on the incredible diversity the world has to offer, and you're depriving your children of the chance to experience other ways of life, cultures, and histories. While it would be ideal to travel to another country for a week or two, I realize that most of us simply can't afford to do that. However, you can achieve similar results just by choosing culturally diverse areas of the United States to visit, such as New Orleans, Miami, or New York. Traveling with an open mind and seeing how others live can be an amazing and life-altering experience.

Another benefit is that vacations can improve your mental skills. For one, it gives you experience with planning and other logic-requiring activities. More importantly, however, the build-up of stress from working too hard and the boredom of sticking to a set routine, day in and day out, interfere with our mental capabilities. We can't think as clearly or as quickly. We may become more forgetful, find it more difficult to listen, and end up making more mistakes. Studies have shown that workplace safety and worker productivity decrease as fewer employees take time off from their jobs.[1] The truth is that our minds need rest, just as much as our bodies do.

Stress reduction is also a good reason to take a vacation. All of us are feeling more and more stress. As mothers, you have to worry not just about yourself, but about your children and the rest of your family as well. That places a lot of strain on you. What's worse is that very few of us know how to deal with stress effectively. Instead, we let it build up until we suffer physical pain, such as headaches or backaches. Or until we reach our breaking point and explode, either in anger or tears. A vacation allows you to break away from those things that cause you the most stress and give you some time to relax.

Vacations are also good for your health. As I already mentioned, they can help you reduce your stress levels, which will also eliminate many problems, such as sleeplessness, aches and pains, skin problems, high blood pressure, upset stomach, depression, and more. There are also long-term health consequences for *not* taking vacations regularly. Researchers have found that women who take vacations less than once every six years have a risk eight times higher than average of dying from a heart attack or heart disease.[2] If you plan to live a long, healthy life, then you'd better work some vacation plans into your busy schedule.

For both working mothers and stay-at-home mothers, another important benefit of vacations is that they reduce burnout. Burnout can be described in many ways, but the main characteristics are feelings of frustration, stress, hopelessness, worthlessness, unimportance, and failure. Many people only associate burnout with working mothers, but the truth is that stay-at-home mothers are just as likely to experience those same symptoms, although they are less likely to share their feelings with others. Burnout is more than just not enjoying your current job, it's a mental and emotional state that makes it difficult for you to function and prevents you from being able to really enjoy your life and your family. A study by the Families and Work Institute in New York found that 55 percent of people who did not take vacation time experienced high levels of burnout.[3] Obviously, breaking your routine and taking some time off to recuperate can dramatically decrease those feelings, which also mean you'll come back feeling more productive and more refreshed.

Although all of these benefits have been important, I think the last two are the most critical reasons that all mothers should take a vacation: vacations strengthen family bonds, and vacations allow *you* to enjoy a real life.

Let's talk about the family bonds first. When you think about your childhood, you hopefully remember many happy times, but I'm guessing that many of the best memories took place during family vacations. That's because those vacations give you and your children a chance to bond, to talk, and to be together without the stresses of work, extracurricular activities, homework, phone calls, or chores. You could all focus on enjoying one another's company and getting to know each other. That's why we tend to treasure those memories from own childhood, and those are the same type of memories we want to give our children.

I'm not suggesting that you spend two weeks in Disneyland or go on a tour of Europe together, although those would be excellent vacation ideas, if you could. Vacations don't need to cost a lot of money or encompass weeks of time in order to give you and your children fulfillment. You might spend the weekend at a nice hotel in your own city or in a nearby town. You might go camping over a three-day weekend. The important thing is that you make the time for all of you to be together without distractions.

Lastly, vacations are a way for you to enjoy your real life. What I mean is that these "Sabbath" moments remind you that you are not just a robot, not just a body producing things. You are a whole child of God. As Americans, we tend to judge our success in terms of our professional lives and our financial accomplishments. That means we often sacrifice large portions of our days to our work. Even when we aren't at work, many of us are so focused on our work that we are never really "tuned in" to our families, or to anything else, for that matter. The truth is, however, that when we look back at our lives, it isn't going to be the memory of those long nights at the office or that successful presentation that warms our hearts. It's going to be the time we spent, with our families and by ourselves, doing the things we truly enjoyed. We can keep working and working, thinking that someday we'll take that vacation of our dreams, but that someday might never come if we don't make time for it now.

That brings me to one final point. We've talked a lot about family vacations, but you also need some time away from the family as well. I know you love your children and your husband, if you have one, but loving them doesn't mean they don't cause you stress. Even though you may not have the ability or the desire to take a week away from your family, there are small ways that you can have private vacations that will provide many of the same benefits we've been discussing. For example, you could hire a babysitter for the afternoon. You could give yourself twenty minutes or more of alone time to work in the garden or soak in a bubble bath. You could send the children to visit their grandparents and invite over some of your friends for a kid-free get-together. You could put on a pair of headphones and listen to your favorite music for half an hour. You could go to the spa for a day of pampering.

Giving yourself private time to do something you enjoy, even for just ten or twenty minutes a day, helps you reduce stress and burnout so you can enjoy life more. No matter how busy and hectic our lives are, we can all find a way to fit a few minutes of relaxation into our days.

Of course, you might find yourself feeling guilty for doing something just for yourself, so remember that taking some time to be by yourself will not only rejuvenate you. It will also help you remember how much you care about your family. When we have people around us every day, we can easily take them for granted and not realize how much they mean to us. Absence can make us thankful for the people who share our lives and our love, so that we are joyful mothers, as well as powerful.

A Balanced Life

A transcendent mother is in balance. She sees with "eternal eyes" and works with "human hands." Successful families require two "accounts"—a financial account, which allows the purchase of goods and services, and a relationship account, which promotes sustainability, bonding, and togetherness. When assets are many and the account balance is large, there is enough to meet the demands that exist in families who are raising children. Life flows joyfully, and motherhood feels great.

At other times, when withdrawals are high, or deposits are low, the relationship account becomes depleted. This is the result of an unbalanced life.

The bank account metaphor helps you remember to make deposits on a regular basis to build up your account. Like the financial bank account, the balance in the mothering account is constantly changing with input and outflow.

Sick children, stress at work, and the stress of Christmas shopping make big withdrawals. Prayer, vacations, and time out alone or with friends are your deposits.

Just like your financial accounts, if the mothering account is consistently overdrawn because its debits are greater than its assets, family bankruptcy may be on the horizon. If you feel this way—and lots of powerful mothers do—the next chapter may help you make some giant deposits into your account.

18

Her Support

One of the most important ways God's love and support are made manifest is through the support of other people. Whether you are single or married, you can't be a powerful mother without the support of other transcendent mothers.

Some of these transcendent mothers have never borne children. They may simply be available to listen to you and strengthen you through prayer. Some may be younger than you and able to help you remember what it's like to be a teenager. Some have raised families of their own and have that oh-so-encouraging long view of childrearing. Some have even raised you! Make a pact with one or more of the powerful mothers in your life to encourage and inspire you along this journey. You'll be amazed at the support you feel in your spirit!

Transcendent Mothers' Pact

> Two people can accomplish more than twice as much as one; they get a better return for their labor. If one person falls, the other can reach out and help. But people who are alone when they fall are in real trouble. (Ecclesiastes 4:9–10)

Mothers' Pacts are deliberate and purposeful. They are strategic plans for gaining support when mothering gets tough. When you are upset, it's hard to hear the still, small voice of the Spirit in you. If you are willing to be humble enough to admit this and call for help, you'll find that help is there. The Transcendent Mothers' Pact gives you access to wisdom that no one human being alone can express. These pacts are formed with women who know and respect what you're trying to do, who support your vision and dreams for your family and your life. It is about humility, knowing that two heads are better than one.

Share a Prayer

No matter how wise or spiritually fit you are, you cannot raise children or complete any mission on your own. An aligned team always outperforms an individual. Part of the pact is that transcendent mothers pray for each other and uphold the highest hopes for each other's children. We pray to see our children, and each other's children, the way God sees them, which is as His children. We pray to see them with eternal eyes so that we waste no time on nonessentials. When we discuss our children, we don't whine and cry over normal childhood behavior. Instead, we give each other breaks, make each other laugh, and remind each other that God's in charge.

As you seek to live the life of a transcendent mother, fellowship with and accountability to another person with the same desire deepens and strengthens your commitment in a powerful way. Pray that the Holy Spirit would bring into your life at least one transcendent mother to share this pact with you. As you continue on your journey as a transcendent mother, know that I, too, take this pact with you in prayer.

In His Name,
Akin

Appendix

TRANSCENDENT MOTHERS' PACT

We, ______________________ and ____________________, being fully desirous of rearing our children to the glory of God, do this ______ day of ______ (month), 20___, commit to each other and to the Holy Spirit that we shall:

- Lift each other and our families to God in prayer daily,
- Reach out humbly for support when human emotion and intellect blocks us from hearing the Guidance of the Holy Spirit
- Hold each other and ourselves accountable for meeting our goals,
- Listen humbly when it is our turn to listen, not with judgment and advice, but with prayer and encouragement.

In gratitude to God, and in the name of Jesus Christ, we say, "Let it now be so."

Amen.

[4] "Life as a Whole," http://www.san.beck.org/Life4-Physical.html

[6] Sagario, Dawn. "Taking Vacations May Save Your Life," Herald.com, 6 July 2004

Notes

Her Body

1. "Breast Milk," http://en.wikipedia.org/wiki/Breast_milk
2. "The Essence of Woman," 1999-2001
3. Keesley, Barbara. *Super Orgasm O*

Her Commitment

1. Akin Merino

Her Rejuvenation

1. ibid.
2. ibid.
3. Ibid.

CPSIA information can be obtained
at www.ICGtesting.com
Printed in the USA
LVOW04s0843210616
493349LV00031B/528/P

9 781682 072103